Visual Sources Series

THE VICTORIAN AGE 1830–1914

Peter Lane

Principal Lecturer in History,
Coloma College of Education, Kent

B. T. BATSFORD LTD London

Uniform with this volume
THE INDUSTRIAL REVOLUTION
THE TWENTIETH CENTURY

First published 1972
© Peter Lane, 1972

Filmset by Keyspools Ltd, Golborne, Lancs.

Printed and bound in Great Britain by
The Anchor Press Ltd, Tiptree, Essex
for the Publishers
B. T. Batsford Ltd, 4 Fitzhardinge Street, London W1

ISBN 7134 1721 8

Acknowledgment

The author and the publishers wish to thank the following for permission to reproduce the illustrations in this book:

Aerofilms Ltd. for Chapter 5, fig. 4; British Rail for Chapter 1, fig. 1; Central Press Photos Ltd. for Chapter 9, fig. 9; the City Art Gallery, Manchester, for Chapter 6, fig. 8; the City of Birmingham Art Gallery for Chapter 4, fig. 8; Glasgow Art Gallery and Museum for Chapter 9, fig. 2; the Greater London Council for Chapter 6, figs. 6 and 7, and Chapter 10, fig. 8; I.C.I. Mond Division for Chapter 2, fig. 4; Illustrated London News for Chapter 4, fig. 4, Chapter 7, fig. 5 and Chapter 10, figs. 1, 2, and 6; London Transport Board for Chapter 4, fig. 7; the Mansell Collection for Chapter 1, figs. 2, 6, 10, Chapter 5, figs. 1(b) 7, 9, Chapter 6, figs. 2 and 3, Chapter 7, figs. 1, 3 and 8, Chapter 8, figs. 4, 6, 9 and 10(b), Chapter 9, figs. 4 and 7, Chapter 10, fig. 4, Chapter 11, fig. 3; Marks and Spencer Ltd. for Chapter 9, fig. 6; the National Monuments Record for Chapter 2, fig. 8 and Chapter 5, fig. 5; the National Portrait Gallery for the portraits of Arnold and Cobden; C. A. Parsons and Co. Ltd., for Chapter 2, fig. 5; Punch for Chapter 1, fig. 8, Chapter 3, figs. 2, 7 and 9 and Chapter 9, fig. 10; G. P. Putnams for Chapter 7, fig. 7; Radio Times Hulton Picture Library for Chapter 1, fig. 5, Chapter 3, figs. 1, 3 and 8, Chapter 4, fig. 5, Chapter 5, fig. 6, Chapter 7, fig. 4, Chapter 8, figs. 2, 3, 7, 8 and 10(a), Chapter 9, figs. 5 and 8, Chapter 10, figs. 5 and 7, Chapter 11, figs. 2, 4, 5, 6, 7 and 8, and for the portraits of Brunel, Chadwick, Gladstone, Disraeli, Florence Nightingale, Bright, Lloyd George, Darwin, Shaftesbury and Peel; Real Photographs Ltd., for Chapter 4, fig. 3; Royal Academy of Arts for Chapter 2, fig. 7; the Science Museum for Chapter 4, figs. 1, 2, 6 and 9; Sheffield City Libraries for Chapter 5, fig. 1(a); University of Reading Museum of Rural Life, for Chapter 3, figs 4 and 5; the Victoria and Albert Museum for Chapter 2, fig. 3; the Wellcome Trustees for Chapter 5, fig. 8.

Contents

List of Illustrations

Introduction

How do we know what life was really like in the past? How do the writers of history books find out? Well, if they are writing about Ancient Times they may have to rely partly on a study of ruins (such as at Stonehenge), of remains dug up by archaeologists (as at Sutton Hoo), of drawings made by cavemen or tools used by Bronze Age workmen. All of these things are 'documents' which tell us something about the past.

If the historian is writing about more modern times he can use written or printed material such as the diaries of Samuel Pepys or the Reports of Royal Commissions into factory conditions in the nineteenth century. Nowadays many of these printed documents have been published so that they can be used by young history students. We no longer have to rely completely on the text-book for our ideas of what life was like in 1500 or 1700 or 1900; we can now read the original documents ourselves.

Most of these collections of documents consist of printed material. This is almost natural since history is, after all, a story and a story is best told in words. But some of these printed documents are very long, the language is often very difficult, so that many of us are unwilling to use them.

It is different with illustrated material; we have an example of the difference if we look at the beginning of the 'Shelter' campaign. There had been dozens of Blue Books and White Papers on the problems of housing in modern Britain; there had been many learned articles, as well as shorter articles in the popular newspapers. But it was only after the BBC had shown the play *Cathy Come Home* that the real plight of the homeless was brought home to people; on the day after the first showing of this film, Des Wilson and a group of young friends decided to do something and 'Shelter' was born. The visual evidence had made much more impact on them than had the written word.

The same is true of the social history of modern Britain. We can, of course, study it through the written document, but we may understand the problem of nineteenth-century poverty much more clearly if we see a contemporary photograph of a group of barefooted children (Book 2, Chapter 9, Picture 8). Similarly, we can read about the problems of old age, but the photograph of the inmates of an Old People's Home in 1880 (Book 2, Chapter 7, Picture 6), brings out clearly what life was really like for these unfortunate people.

Of course the picture document, like the written document, has to be used very carefully by the historian. He has to ask questions about it, compare one picture with another, compare the evidence presented by the photograph with the evidence collected elsewhere – in the written word for example. It would be bad history, for instance, to conclude that all working-class people were very poor in 1900, yet this is certainly the evidence of some pictures (Book 2, Chapter 7, Pictures 7 and 9). But these pictures do not tell the whole story because there were other working-class people who were well off at this time (Book 2, Chapter 8, Picture 2). The job of the historian is to weigh up one piece of evidence with another before he begins to write his story.

In these three volumes I have tried to show how the historian works; there are questions about the pictures which will help to bring out the significance of the evidence presented; there are other questions which ask the Young Historian to compare one piece of evidence with another; there are questions which direct the Young Historian's attention to plays, novels or other written documents.

I have also tried to offer the Young Historian a variety of work – painting, letter-writing, reading – which will help him to recreate for himself, by his own imagination, what the past was like. These questions are not meant to be a final, complete list; there are many other questions to be asked on the pictures and many other kinds of work that might be tackled. The questions, like the picture-documents, are only illustrative and not exhaustive.

1 Living Standards, 1830–1914

My income and yours

In *David Copperfield*, Mr Micawber said: 'Annual income twenty pounds, annual expenditure nineteen pounds, nineteen and six – result happiness. Annual income twenty pounds, annual expenditure twenty pounds, ought and sixpence – result misery'. Each of us knows that Mr Micawber was right – we cannot spend more than we earn. Our personal income is one of the main factors which decides the standard of living at which we live – what kind of house, clothes, furniture and food we have, what holidays we enjoy, how we travel and spend our leisure time. If we have a small income we enjoy a lower standard of living than people who have a high income.

Our income is one factor which decides our living standards. Another factor is our own decision on how we spend that income. If we decide to save a good deal of our income then we will have a lower standard of living than if we had spent it all. Similarly, if we decide to spend a lot of money on clothes then we will have less to spend on holidays.

The nation's income

Every day the people of this country use their *labour* and, with the help of different kinds of machinery or equipment (or *capital*) they produce certain goods or provide certain services. In some cases this produce is easy to measure; we can go to a brickyard and count the number of bricks which the men have made in a day. In other cases it is difficult to measure accurately what a person has produced at the end of a day. How, for example, can we measure the output of a teacher or nurse?

One way is to add up the incomes which people receive for the work they do – whether producing something like bricks or cars, or providing some service such as teachers, nurses, clerks and many others do. The total of their incomes is the *nation's income* – and is a measure of the goods and services provided by the nation.

Some nations have a high income – the USA in 1970 had an average income of about £800 per person (man, woman and child). In Britain the average is about £500. In India it is about £30. The main reason for differences between these countries is the difference in their industrial development. America has gone further along the road of industrial progress; her workpeople produce more wealth each working hour than do the people of Britain – who, in turn, produce much more than do the people in India.

National income and living standards

The USA has a very high national income – and the people of the USA enjoy a very high standard of living. They have more cars, better roads, more university students, bigger newspapers and more varied food than the British have. Both the Americans and the British have more telephones, schoolteachers and holidays than the Indians can afford. As countries become more industrialized so the nation's income rises – and so does the standard of living of its inhabitants.

Dividing the nation's income

We have seen that the size of our personal income is only one factor in deciding our standard of living; another important factor is the decisions we make about the use of that income. In the same way the nation's total income is only one factor in deciding the nation's standard of living; another important factor is the answer given to the question: 'How is the national income to be divided up?' There are many ways in which we might spend part or indeed all of the income; we might spend more on defence or war, or build more offices, hospitals and schools – and fewer houses, bridges and factories. We might spend more on food and less on machinery, more on entertainment and less on education.

Social history and the nation's income

In this volume we will see that the nation's wealth increased as a result of the second stage of the industrial revolution; we will also see the various ways in which this increased income was spent. In the third volume we will take the story up to our own time and notice both a continuing increase in the nation's income and the changes in the ways in which it was spent.

Britain in 1830

The first stage of the industrial revolution had been completed by 1830 when the first public railways were being built. This marked the beginning of the second stage of the industrial revolution. By 1830 Watt's steam engine and

1   Crimple viaduct

2 The first meeting of the London School Board

3 Graph showing the output of coal, iron and steel in the United Kingdom between 1750 and 1954

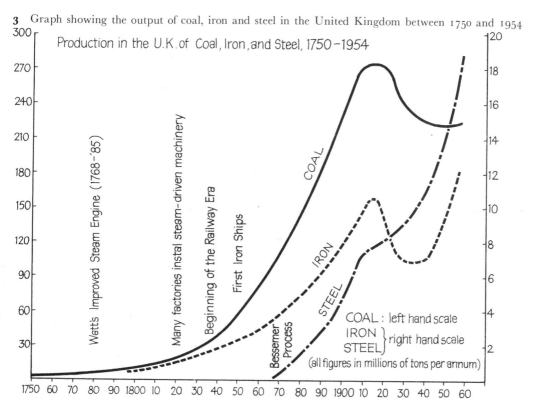

Production in the U.K. of Coal, Iron, and Steel, 1750–1954

Watts Improved Steam Engine (1768–'85)

Many factories instal steam-driven machinery

Beginning of the Railway Era

First Iron Ships

Bessemer Process

COAL

IRON

STEEL

COAL : left hand scale
IRON } right hand scale
STEEL }
(all figures in millions of tons per annum)

1750 60 70 80 90 1800 10 20 30 40 50 60 70 80 90 1900 10 20 30 40 50 60

4 Preparing tea—a painting by Jane Bowker

5 *Below* Charabanc outing—the Manchester trade picnic, 1912

6 Inside a poor East-End home about 1900

various inventions in the textile industry had led to the growth of large factories surrounded by large towns. The nation's income was growing. Some of this increase was being set aside to build new factories, new machines and new railways. Another part was being taken by the industrial and merchant middle-class to provide large houses and a high standard of living. There was little left for the working-class who had a poor quality of life – in terms of food, housing, wages, clothing or living conditions.

The continuing industrial revolution

With the building of the new railway system, with its thousands of miles of lines, many engines, hundreds of wagons and many bridges (Picture 1, and see also Chapter 4) there was a huge increase in the demand for coal and iron (to make the lines and engines). As the railway system was completed, the demand for coal continued, to provide the fuel to drive the engines (Chapter 2, Picture 1, and Picture 3 here). The boom in the demand for iron (Chapter 2, Picture 2) continued as overseas countries increased their demand for British goods – for our engineering products, our coal and later our ships (Chapter 2, Picture 3). By 1851 Britain had become the workshop of the world, a position she was to hold until the end of the nineteenth century.

7 Bentall's new shop at Kingston

National income and social progress

The increased output of coal, iron, textiles and other products meant an increase in the size of the nation's income. Some of this was set aside to provide new factories and machines, and some of it was used to help industrialise overseas countries which borrowed money in Britain. Another part of the income was taken to provide a high living standard for the growing number of middle-class people (Pictures 4 and 7, and Chapter 2, Pictures 6 and 8), and for the skilled workers who used their trade unions to force industrialists to give them higher wages (Picture 5, and Chapter 4, Picture 8; and Chapter 9, Picture 5).

By the end of the period the government was taking part of the increased income (by taxation) to provide better living conditions in our towns (Chapter 5, Picture 4; and Chapter 6, Pictures 6 and 7) as well as to pay for Factory Inspectors (Chapter 10, Picture 4). More money was being spent on education (Chapter 10, Pictures 7 and 5) while a start had been made on providing old-age pensions (Chapter 7, Picture 8, unemployment benefit (Chapter 5), as well as an early form of National Health Service (Picture 6). A wealthier nation could afford to set aside some of its wealth to provide these social services.

The third stage of the industrial revolution

By the end of the nineteenth century a number of new industries had been started, for example chemicals (Chapter 2, Picture 4) and electrical engineering

8 Old Age Pensions—'The New Year's Gift'.

(Chapter 2, Picture 5). In such industries the hourly output of each workman was much greater than the hourly output of a workman in one of the older industries and this allowed the nation's income to grow even more rapidly than it had in the past. Unfortunately, Britain was slow to take up some of these new industries. By 1914 Germany and the USA had overtaken Britain in the production of coal and iron and steel (Picture 9). They had also taken a more serious interest in the development of the newer industries than had Britain whose industrialists seemed to be satisfied that 'what had made us great will continue to keep us great', and who were reluctant to give up their interest in coal, cotton and iron in favour of an interest in some of the newer industries.

This foreign competition meant that Britain lost some of her overseas markets

9 Graph of the growth of Germany and the USA.

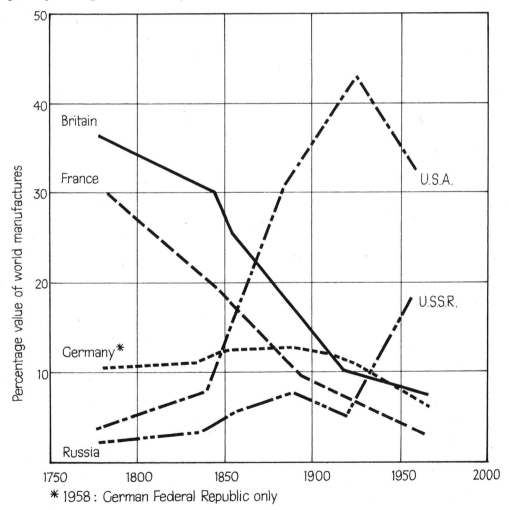

* 1958: German Federal Republic only

Percentage of world's industrial production

as some of our former markets were taken over by Germany or the USA. We also faced a flood of goods from these countries invading the domestic market so that by the end of the nineteenth century unemployment had become a regular feature of British life (Picture 10, and Chapter 2, Picture 7).

Social structure in 1914
There were many rich people in the Britain which entered the First World War; for them, life was good (Chapter 5, Picture 5; Chapter 7, Picture 1; Chapter 9, Pictures 2 and 3; see also Chapter 11). There were many skilled workers who gained from rising wages and falling prices (Chapter 3, Picture 6) and whose standard of living rose almost continually throughout this period. But there were many – about one-third of the population in 1914 – who did not have sufficient income to provide enough food, clothing or shelter to keep themselves properly. These are the people described in Jack London's novel *The People of the Abyss*, whose existence was first revealed on a large scale by the work of Charles Booth and Seebohm Rowntree. The nation's income was still not being divided in a sufficiently fair way – too few people got a great deal, too many people got very little.

1 The Young Historian

1   Picture 1 shows the Crimple viaduct built in 1848. Can you say what skills are required for such building? Why were there many such bridges built in the nineteenth-century Britain? Are there any near your home town?

2   There was an increase in output of coal during the nineteenth century. Which areas of the country benefited by this increase? How were they affected when the Royal Navy and the Merchant Navy began to use oil instead of coal after 1900?

3   In Picture 4 the children and the mother are waiting for the father to come home on the train (in the background). What sort of people are they? Compare this picture with Picture 6, and write a letter from one child to another about their lives.

4   In Picture 5 you can see working-class people preparing to go on an outing. Why were such outings not possible in 1830? There were many such outings at the end of the period (1830–1914). What does this tell you about the standard of living of working-class people?

5   Give five examples of ways in which life was better for working-class people in 1914 than it had been in 1830.

6   In Picture 7 you can see one of the many huge shops built at the end of the nineteenth century. What sort of people used these shops? What do these shops tell you about the living standards of the British people?

7   Picture 8 shows one of the Liberal Government's social measures. Why could governments afford to provide a welfare state in 1910 and not in 1830? Find out what the Liberals did between 1906 and 1914 for (i) the old, (ii) the sick, and (iii) the unemployed.

8   In Picture 9 you can see evidence of increasing competition from Germany and the USA. How do these figures help to explain the rise in the numbers of people unemployed in Britain at the end of the period? Which areas suffered most from this unemployment? (See also Question 2.)

2 Industrial Change

The factory system

Throughout the period there was an almost continuous spread of the factory system; at first this had affected only the textile industry, and many industries continued to be 'domestic' – nail-making, for instance, was done in Staffordshire homes until the 1870s. But gradually the advantages of the factory system were realised and more and more industries lost their domestic character as industrialists provided larger machines in factories. This led to a continuous growth in Britain's towns; by 1851 over half the population lived in towns and less than half lived in the countryside; by 1901 over three-quarters of the people lived in large towns and the countryside was almost deserted.

However, domestic industries existed even at the end of the period. Dressmaking, for example, box-making and other industries were done in people's homes. In these industries conditions of pay and hours of work were often much worse than in the factories which were subject to Factory Acts and visits from Factory Inspectors.

Industrial growth

Throughout the period there was a continuous increase in the demand for coal (Chapter 1, Picture 3, and Picture 1 here). Coal was needed in the iron

1 Working the ten-yard coal seam

2 Pouring metal in an iron foundry

3 The industry of the Tyne—a painting by W. Bell Scott

and steel industries (Picture 2), which also continued to develop as iron· and steel replaced timber in building, machine-making and shipbuilding (Picture 3). It was also used as a domestic fuel in larger houses (Chapter 5, Picture 5) and as a source of power in the new railways (Chapter 4, Pictures 3, 4 and 8). Most industries used coal to drive their machines (Picture 4) while the new gas companies used coal to provide them with their fuel.

Coal, iron and shipbuilding were industries in which men used a good deal of physical effort in their work. There was little room for the old, the weak, or for women in such industries – although women found plenty of work in other industries (Picture 9; and Chapter 8, Picture 9). These were the 'staple' industries which provided most of the wealth of mid-nineteenth century Britain, from whom the rest of the world bought coal, machines, railway systems, as well as manufactured consumer goods such as textiles.

Towards the end of the nineteenth century a series of new inventions and discoveries led to the development of new industries. One was the chemical industry (Picture 4) in which Alfred Mond laid the foundations of what has since become Imperial Chemical Industries. Another was electrical engineering (Picture 5) in which men like Parsons, Swan and Napier helped to develop a new form of power for driving ships and machines. A third was the car industry (Chapter 4, Picture 6) in which British and foreign inventors together developed a new form of road transport.

In these new industries there is less emphasis on the physical power of the workman, and more on the work of scientists, of complicated machinery and of trained workpeople. One effect of this was the growth in the number of qualified workpeople (Picture 6); these engineers or technologists had to be trained in colleges or universities – which led to a demand for an expansion in state education (Chapter 10). When they went to work, these people helped to design new machines, invent new methods of production, discover new products – all of which helped to increase the size of the nation's income.

4 Brunner and Mond works – the first works of the chemical firm which became I.C.I.

5 Heavy machinery shop at Heaton works, Newcastle, in 1901

Companies

Such machines and inventions were very costly. In the early nineteenth century an individual could either hope to save enough out of his wages to set himself up as a factory owner or borrow from friends the money needed to make a start as an industrialist. But the new industries were too costly for money to be raised in this casual way. The new industralists had to ask the rich middle- and upper-classes to lend them many thousands of pounds to help them start their new industries. This led to the development of the joint-stock companies with their large Head offices (Picture 8). Both in the offices and in the work of the highly-qualified technologists there was room for women workers – if only they could become qualified and if they could break down the idea that a woman's place was in the home.

Britain's decline

In the 1850s Britain had earned the title of 'the workshop of the world'. The country of Watt and Arkwright, of Stephenson and Brunel, had been the first to enter on the industrial revolution. Towards the end of the nineteenth century, however, Britain lost her lead in the industrial race. Using more and better machinery in new coal mines, both Germany and the USA produced more and cheaper coal in 1913 than did Britain. In larger and more mechanised steelworks they produced cheaper steel. More seriously, these countries invested heavily in the new industries while Britain seemed content to jog along with the industrial system that had made her great in the past. While the national income of this country grew, it grew less rapidly than did the incomes of Germany and the USA. This meant that in the future these countries would have more money for investing in more modern industries, more to spend on the welfare of their people and on raising their living standards.

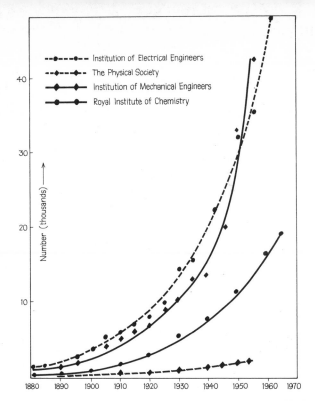

6 Graph showing the increasing number of technicians employed from the end of the last century.

7 Unemployed. Before the advent of the Welfare State unemployment meant desperate poverty for the workman and his family.

8 Head Office of Pears Soap Company in 1888. This was one of the first companies to open a London Head Office.

9 Women workers in a pen-grinding factory.

In 1970 we can see the result of this nineteenth-century development in Germany and the USA. However, even in the nineteenth century, Britain suffered from this growth of foreign competition. Some of our export trades suffered as our overseas buyers went to Germany and the USA for their needs. Unemployment in the coal, iron, textile, shipbuilding and other industries grew, so that it is estimated that in the last twenty years of the century about twelve per cent of British workers were unemployed. At first the government did nothing about this; workmen were expected to provide out of their savings for periods of unemployment. If they had no savings then they had to go to a private charity (Chapter 7, Picture 6), or to the workhouse (Chapter 7, Picture 4). Not until 1911 did the government begin to provide some unemployment benefit for some of those who could not find work.

2 The Young Historian

1 Look at Pictures 1 and 2. What dangers can you see to workmen in Picture 2? Why were many miners killed in the nineteenth century?

2 In *Rape of the Fair Country* (Chapters 18 and 22) Alexander Cordell gives a description of an accident at an iron works. Read this and then draw your own picture of such an accident.

3 Look at Pictures 1, 2 and 3. Why was this sort of work particularly unsuitable for women and children?

4 Look at Picture 6. What does it tell you about the type of industry that was growing in late Victorian Britain? How does it help to explain the need for an increase in the number of children going on to education after the age of eleven?

5 Picture 8 shows the interior of the London offices of a national soap firm. Find out the name of three other firms which have their national headquarters in London. Why did such offices increase the chance of women finding a job?

6 Write a letter from a girl employed at one of the new offices (Picture 8) to one of the girls in the factory (Picture 9).

7 Pictures 4 and 5 illustrate the growth of a new type of industry in the latter part of the nineteenth century. Imagine that you are an old man in 1900 and write a letter to your grandson who is just beginning his working life in one of the new industries, telling him how lucky he is.

8 Find out more about the work of (i) Joseph Swan, (ii) C. A. Parsons, (iii) Dunlop.

3 Agriculture

In Book 1, Chapter 3, we saw that the agrarian revolution of the late nineteenth century had led to the development of larger farms on which improved machinery and methods were used by fewer workers to produce more and cheaper food. We saw that the rich farmers and their landlords used their political power to get Parliament to pass the Corn Laws (1815), which guaranteed a sale for the output of the British farmers, often at a very high price.

Anti-Corn Law League

In 1839 Richard Cobden and John Bright helped to form the Anti-Corn Law League with its headquarters in Manchester but with branches throughout the country. Cobden and Bright represented the manufacturers – who had been given the vote in 1832 (Chapter 6) – and who believed in Free Trade. They wanted no tariffs on imports into Britain and no duties on British exports. They argued that if tariffs were removed then raw materials would be cheaper, manu-

1 Signing an Anti-Corn Law League petition

2 The Rebecca Riots

factured goods would be cheaper, overseas sales would be greater and Britain would prosper. In the case of corn they argued that if foreign corn could be imported into Britain this would keep the price of food down, so that there would be less demand for increased wages; profits could then rise so that manufacturers could invest more money in machinery, thus making Britain a richer country.

Throughout the country they gained the support of middle- and working-class people who gladly signed their petitions for the abolition of the Corn Laws (Picture 1). Some people saw the League as part of a general demand for greater freedom – from Church tithes, toll gates, restrictions on Catholics and Jews, and so on (Picture 2). By 1846 the League had persuaded Prime Minister Peel to abolish the Corn Laws. This move was denounced by Disraeli, who argued that the British farmer would be ruined, that agriculture was being sacrificed to the cotton industry and that the landed aristocracy would fade away to be replaced by the new industrial middle-class. In fact, for twenty years after the

3 The Farmer's Friend—a cartoon by Richard Doyle

repeal the British farmer continued to prosper (Picture 3). An increasing town population demanded more and more food from fewer and fewer farmers; an increasingly wealthy middle- and working-class demanded a greater variety of food; the new railway system made it possible for the British farmer to supply these needs.

During these so-called golden years (1846–70) the British farmer invested in new machinery (Picture 4) and through various agricultural societies and journals learned about scientific farming. At Rothamsted, Sir John Lawes started a model farm where he experimented with chemical fertilisers, new strains of seeds, and new breeds of animals. British farmers profited from these experiments.

Depression

However, while this was going on in Britain, the prairies of America, the pampas of Argentina and the plains of Australia and New Zealand were being developed – often as a result of the building of a railway or a harbour by a British contractor. In these new lands, rents were cheap or non-existent, farms were large and had to be mechanised so that output per man was very high. By 1870 the steam ship had been developed which made it possible to bring American corn to Britain in only six days; in the 1880s refrigerated shipping was developed which allowed the importation of frozen meat from Argentina and Australasia.

4　An early threshing machine

5 Haymaking at Locking, 1905

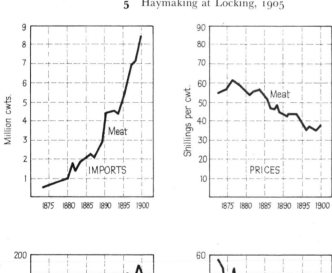

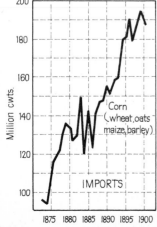

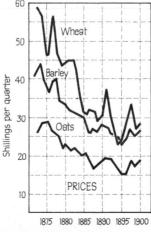

6 Graphs of price falls and of rising imports

7 Bad weather and the farmer—*Punch* cartoon

A CRUMB OF COMFORT.

JONATHAN. "THEY *DU* SAY WE SENT YOU THIS DARN'D WEATHER! DON'T KNOW 'BOUT THA ANYHOW, I GUESS WE'LL SEND YOU THE CORN!!!"

FARMER BULL. "THANK'EE KINDLY, JONATHAN, BUT I'D RATHER HA' DONE WITHOUT BOTH!!!"

8 *Below* Loading cabbages for market in the early 1900s

9 (a) and (b) Living conditions—in the pigsty and the labourers' cottage—*Punch*, 1863

This led to a dramatic fall in food prices in Britain (Picture 6). It was of immense benefit to the town worker and to the middle classes; their wages and incomes remained steady, their cost of living fell. This meant that they had more money to spend on other things – clothes, holidays, housing, education, furniture, and so on – so that the nation's standard of living rose during this so-called 'depression'.

But for the farmer it meant ruin. Some farmers were already ruined by a series of bad harvests and outbreaks of diseases among animals (Picture 7). The import of cheap, foreign food was the last straw. Many gave up the task of farming altogether. Others changed to vegetable farming (Picture 8) providing for the townspeople the products that could not be so easily imported.

Many people lost their jobs as a result of this depression in agriculture. They left behind their cottages (Picture 9) and went to live in the towns where they hoped to find work. For many the change to town life was an improvement on what they had known in the past. Although they lost their village community (Picture 5) they gained the benefits of living in towns where wages were higher, living standards were better and where there were many more opportunities of education and entertainment (Chapters 10 and 11).

3 The Young Historian

1   Look at Picture 1 and Picture 6. Many working-class people supported the Anti-Corn Law League in the 1840s. How did they gain from the falls in food prices after 1870?

2   There was a lot of unemployment in Victorian Britain (Chapter 2, Picture 7) but for many people there was full time work and rising wage rates. At the same time prices fell (Question 1). Can you say what effect this had on the standard of living of the working classes? Suggest three ways in which they might have spent their extra money.

3   Look at Picture 4. Why did such machines lead to a fall in the numbers employed on Britain's farms? How did they affect the size of Britain's national income?

4   Paint either (i) haymaking (Picture 5) or (ii) threshing (Picture 4).

5   Look at Picture 8. Why was there a more varied and cheaper supply of food in late Victorian towns than in such towns in 1830? How did this affect the health of the population?

6   Picture 9 shows that living conditions in the countryside remained at a low level. Write a letter from a town child in 1900 telling your country cousin about the good life in the town.

7   Look again at Pictures 7, 8 and 9. Who suffered most from the agricultural depression after 1870? Find out three reasons for this depression.

8   Not all farmers suffered; many had become more scientifically minded. Find out more about (i) Richard Cobden and the Anti-Corn Law League, (ii) Disraeli's opposition to this League (Picture 7). Why did British farmers not suffer a depression immediately after 1846?

4 Transport

Railways

The first public railway line had been opened in 1825 (Book 1, Chapter 4), and between 1830 and 1850 over 6,000 miles of railway lines were laid in Britain. As we have seen (Chapters 1 and 2) this led to an increased demand for coal and iron; it also led to the growth in the number of engineers who had to supervise the building of the railway system (Picture 1), the construction of the hundreds of bridges (Chapter 1, Picture 1) and the design and building of the many engines. The railway companies were among the first of the joint-stock companies which invited the richer people of the country to lend them money — to buy land, pay the builders, buy materials and equipment. In the 1830s and 1840s huge sums of money were borrowed by the railway companies to be spent in various ways, all of which led to increased employment in many industries.

Among the main gainers from the building of railways were the British farmers who were now able to sell their produce over a much wider area than before (compare Book 1, Chapter 3, Picture 1; and Book 2, Chapter 3, Picture 8).

1 Building the railway—Tring cutting, 1837

This wider distribution of food was of immediate benefit to the townspeople – the middle- and skilled working-classes who could afford to buy the milk and meat, the vegetables and cheese. This had its effects on people's health, which was also improved as they were able to live further away from their place of work, travelling thereto by train (Chapter 1, Picture 4, and Picture 4 here). The middle-classes also used the railways to take their children to the new boarding schools (Book 1, Chapter 10, Picture 1), and to get away for holidays (Chapter 11, Picture 4). The working-class could not take a holiday, but used the railways for an afternoon's outing into the countryside or to visit the seaside (Picture 8).

Coal, iron and engineering industrialists got high profits from their industries, which expanded with the building of the railways. Other businessmen also gained; some used the railways to distribute newspapers and so the national press developed. Others used the railways to distribute their goods to the shops (Chapter 1, Picture 7) and so large firms appeared which made soap and other products to be sold all over the country (Chapter 2, Picture 8).

British railway builders such as Thomas Brassey were invited by private companies or by governments to build railway systems in Europe and America. Most of these borrowed money on the London Stock Exchange for the purchase of British materials and equipment, so adding to the boom in British industry. When they began to pay interest on this borrowed money they provided the British people with an increase to the national income which was 'unearned' compared with the income earned by producing some article.

Road transport

By 1830 the stagecoach had reached a peak of perfection (Book 1, Chapter 4) in speed and comfort – but this was a costly method of travel which only the very rich could afford. Many of these rich people had their own carriages for transport to and from their own homes – to work, to the theatre, or to parties. Less wealthy people who did not have their own carriages might hire a horse-drawn cab, or use one of the horse-drawn buses (Picture 5) which had been started in London by Thomas Shillibeer in 1829, and whose example had been imitated in most towns by the end of the century. For one shilling people could travel about three miles, which made shopping and visiting a more comfortable business for the people who could afford it.

Less well-off people welcomed the development of the electric tram (Picture 7) on which they travelled on wooden benches for 1d or 2d compared with 1/– on the horse-drawn bus. The tram was quicker and less dirty than the horse bus; it was larger and carried more people. Lines were laid in most towns, and people were able to live away from their place of work since they could travel quickly and cheaply from their homes. The building of suburbs in and around our large towns followed the development first of suburban railway systems (and in London of the Underground), and then of the tramway system.

2 An early bicycle of 1890

In 1891 the first electrically-driven tram appeared, and in 1901 many towns and cities had abolished the horse-drawn tram in favour of the more efficient electrically-driven one. C. F. G. Masterman wrote:

> Eight years ago, when I first went to live in a poor district of South London, ... our sole communication with London over-the-bridge was a few erratic horse omnibuses, and lines of slow-moving two-horse trams, which diverged fan-like to the bases of the various bridges. Here, at evening, a tired, indignant crowd fought silently for entrance into each successive conveyance; the young and the old were squeezed and occasionally trampled under. The crowded tram jogged off quietly into the night. By the dim light of two odorous oil lamps, we contemplated dismally the dismal countenance of our neighbours. Half-an-hour afterwards, or perhaps three-quarters, we were deposited ... (near) ... our home.

3 A coal train

4   A rush hour train at Victoria station, 1865. People were already commuting to work in the cities from homes in the suburbs.

5   Horse buses in the Strand, 1887.

Several experiments had been made with a bicycle (or two-wheeled cycle). By the 1890s the safety bicycle (Picture 2) had been developed and the later invention of the pneumatic tyre by John Dunlop of Belfast meant that riding was more comfortable. The bicycle was, at first, an expensive machine afforded only by the very rich; Prime Minister Balfour apologised to the House of Commons on one occasion for appearing with an arm broken in a cycling accident. Well-to-do people used the cycle to get out into the countryside; they formed cycling clubs – and Mrs Bloomer designed a dress which 'respectable' ladies could wear while cycling. As R. D. Blumenfeld noted in his diary in 1900:

> Ladies who persist in riding bicycles in long skirts must expect to get hurt. I saw a handsome Junoesque figure today dressed in laces and flounces, riding a bicycle in Sloane Street. Her skirt became entangled and she came down with a crash. My tailor tells me that women flatly refuse to wear short skirts for fear of exposing their legs.

The mass production of the bicycle led to a fall in price so that it could be bought by working people – who used it for leisure as well as to get themselves to and from work. Shop assistants were provided with special bicycles to help them deliver goods over a wider area.

Most social improvements begin with richer people. They were the first to live away from factories, to enjoy holidays at the seaside or abroad, to have comfortable houses. Slowly the improvement made its way down the social ladder as more and more people were able to afford what was once only a rich person's pleasure. Nowhere is this clearer than in the case of the motor car which made its first appearance on British roads in the 1890s. At first (Picture 6) this horseless carriage was a hand-built, expensive thing; its very name suggests that it was meant for those people who previously had been able to afford a carriage and horses. Not until the 1920s did ordinary people begin to think of owning a car.

6   A Lanchester car, 1897

7 Electric tramcars drove the horse buses off the roads

The steamship

In the middle of the nineteenth century the USA was the world's largest ship-building country, mainly because of a plentiful supply of cheap timber. The use first of iron and later of the lighter steel in shipbuilding, gave Britain an advantage over other countries; in the 1860s she was the world's leading iron and steel producing country, so it is not surprising that she also became an important shipbuilding country. As metal replaced wood in shipbuilding so ships could be of greater length and carry more people and/or goods. This led to the search for a new way of driving the ships since sail could not propel these larger vessels. Steam engines had been used on wooden ships in the Clyde in 1809; experiments with seagoing ships led to the building of the *Royal William* (1837), the first ship to cross the Atlantic by steam. Once again Britain gained from this development; her engineers were the first to build steam engines – for use in factories and railway trains. It is not surprising that they were the first to build steam engines to drive ships, so that by the 1900s Britain was building about three-quarters of all the world's ships.

35

This led to the development of major industries along the Tyne and the Clyde, where thousands of men were employed in shipbuilding. It also continued the demand for iron, steel and coal – both to build and to run the ships. British farmers, however, suffered from this development (Chapter 3).

Air travel

Sir George Cayley, a versatile Yorkshire squire, made the world's first model glider in 1804 and went on perfecting the apparatus until 1852, when he built a full-scale glider and gave his reluctant coachman a trip in it. By 1900 a considerable body of theory and practice had been acquired in the science of aeronautics. In 1899 Britain's glider pioneer, Percy Pilcher, was killed near Market Harborough. He was on the verge of actually powering his glider with an oil engine, and thus the first true aeroplane might well have been British.

In 1903 the two brothers, Orville and Wilbur Wright, built the first practical aeroplane. It was, in effect, two wings consisting of canvas-covered metal struts, with a front-and-tail-plane for stability. A light motor-cycle engine drove two propellers. It flew for twelve seconds at ten mph. By 1914 some models could touch 100 mph and perform enthralling manoeuvres such as flying upside-down.

It was not until 1906 that an aeroplane took off in Europe (Santos-Dumont's flight in Paris) and 1907 that a flight was made in Great Britain. This was made by the American, Cody, at Farnborough, Hampshire. The first Englishman to fly in England was A. V. Roe, who flew at Brooklands race track (Surrey) in 1908. In 1909 the Frenchman Bleriot flew over the English Channel in $35\frac{1}{2}$ minutes and thus demonstrated in a dramatic way the great possibilities of aeroplanes. The main British event of this era was the London to Manchester air race (1910), with a prize of £10,000 offered to the winner. Next year an American, Rodgers, flew across the USA in forty-nine days (four days' actual flying time) – an heroic effort, especially if one remembers that he was the victim of vicious attacks by an eagle at one point!

8 An excursion train to Brighton, 1859

9 The first flight, December 1903

In 1913 Londoners flocked to Hendon where demonstration flights and trips for the public provided a new and exciting form of leisure. In ten years the plane had developed from a frail, powered glider into a powerful machine capable of diving, soaring and somersaulting at speed.

In August 1914, the First World War broke out, and the aeroplane entered on a new phase of rapid development.

4 The Young Historian

1   Look at Picture 4. Can you see three different tools being carried? What occupations did the people carrying these have?

2   What other evidence can you see in Picture 4 that the people leaving the train are working-class? Compare this picture with Picture 4 in Chapter 1. Can you suggest differences between these people and the husband of the family in the suburban house?

3   In Picture 4 in Chapter 1 and again in Picture 4 here we have evidence of people travelling to work by train. How did people travel to work before the coming of the railway? Why in particular had working-class people got to live near their factory?

4   Write a letter describing your first day in a new suburban home to someone still living in the old part of the industrial town.

5   Picture 8 shows an excursion. Why did such trains alter people's use of their free time? Write a letter describing a child's first train journey and visit to the seaside.

6   Trains carried goods as well as people (Picture 3). Can you say why railways were important to (i) fishermen in Grimsby. (ii) farmers in Cornwall, (iii) housewives shopping in a large town?

7   Make your own painting of either Pictures 4, 5 or 8.

8   Look at the car in Picture 6. What sort of people bought these first cars? Can you suggest why this car was called 'The Horseless Carriage'? Why was travel in these cars very uncomfortable?

5 Health and Housing

Town growth

When industrialists built factories or opened coal mines in the late eighteenth and early nineteenth centuries there were no laws to restrict their freedom to do as they pleased. When they built houses for their workers these industrialists spent as little as they could on building as many houses as possible (see Book 1, Chapter 5). The poorly-paid workers crowded into these small, insanitary hovels, where often they could only afford to rent a room or two. The absence of any system of refuse collection, street cleaning, sanitary provision or proper water supply made these working-class areas a seed-bed for disease (Picture 2). A poorly-clad, poorly-fed population was frequently attacked by epidemics, including at least three major outbreaks of cholera (Picture 2).

Poverty and Health

Even before 1830 public-spirited philanthropists had been concerned at such living conditions (Book 1, Chapter 5). In 1834 the government had reformed the Poor Law system (Chapter 7) and appointed Edwin Chadwick to head the first centralised administrative machine – the Poor Law Commission. Chadwick and his Commissioners found that there was a direct link between poverty and insanitary living conditions; they found that some families had to go into the workhouse because the father had died; and that others applied for poor relief when the father was sick for a long period. Chadwick organised the first inquiry into living conditions in British towns and in 1842 reported that over half the

1 Housing (a) the town – Sheffield (*below left*):
(b) inside a one-roomed house in the 1880s
(*right*)

children died before they reached the age of five – i.e. before they went to work. His inquiry showed that the average expectation of life among the working-class was only seventeen years and for the middle-classes only twenty-five years. Each year thousands of people were dying because of the insanitary conditions in British towns.

2   Cholera notice

CHOLERA.

THE
DUDLEY BOARD OF HEALTH,
HEREBY GIVE NOTICE, THAT IN CONSEQUENCE OF THE
Church-yards at Dudley

Being so full, no one who has died of the
CHOLERA will be permitted to be buried
after *SUNDAY* next, (To-morrow) in either
of the Burial Grounds of *St. Thomas's, or
St. Edmund's*, in this Town.

All Persons who die from CHOLERA, must for the future
be buried in the Church-yard at Nethertor

BOARD of HEALTH, DUDLEY.

Government regulation on town building

In 1848 the government passed the first Public Health Act which allowed a
Central Board of Health in London to appoint local Boards of Health in towns
where the death rate was over 23 per 1,000 inhabitants. This was opposed by
the liberal philosophers who thought it was an interference with people's freedom to live as they chose; it was also opposed by people who resented paying a
health rate to provide for refuse collection or the building of drains. But each
succeeding government passed more and more Acts concerning the nation's
health. Slowly there came into being a body of Medical Officers of Health,
Sanitary Inspectors, Building Inspectors, to administer these new laws which
compelled builders to instal a proper sanitary system in each new house, to
provide pavements and paved streets, and to lay on a water supply. Under the
supervision of these officials thousands of houses (Picture 4) were built where
working-class people could lead a healthier life than hitherto.

Private enterprise and housing

Some industrialists had a sense of responsibility towards their workpeople.
Titus Salt was a Bradford textile manufacturer who had been appalled at the

4 Bye law housing at Middlesborough, Yorkshire

5 'The Towers' Leeds

way in which some of his workpeople lived. He built a new town, Saltaire, where he provided (at reasonable rents) decent houses, working men's clubs, parks, schools, churches, museums, libraries and other amenities. His example was copied by others – the Cadbury family built the model town of Bournville for their workers, the soap manufacturer Lever built Port Sunlight. These men proved that it was possible to provide decent living standards for working people; they also proved that in such living conditions the people's health improved and they lived a longer life.

Other philanthropists tried to provide decent housing for working-class people. George Peabody was an American who had been horrified at living conditions in London. He provided the money for the building of many Peabody Buildings (Picture 9). While these might appear barrack-like to our eyes, to the workers who went to live there such buildings offered room, light, air, water, and sanitation and facilities for washing and drying clothes.

Improved health

Successive governments passed laws concerning house building, slum clearance, water supplies, and so on. Many local authorities (Chapter 6) had taken advantage of these laws and begun to provide decent living conditions for some of

THE DAWN OF HOPE.

Mr. LLOYD GEORGE'S National Health Insurance Bill provides for the insurance of the Worker in case of Sickness.

Support the Liberal Government
in their policy of
SOCIAL REFORM.

6 Lloyd George's Insurance poster, 1911

7 Over London by rail, by Gustave Doré, 1872

8 Louis Pasteur in his laboratory

the people (Chapter 6, Picture 6). As skilled workers earned higher wages they themselves began to save in the newly-formed Building Societies, and many bought their own houses (Chapter 8, Picture 2). After 1870 these workers were able to afford a better diet as food prices fell (Chapter 3, Picture 6), so that the health of many families improved. In 1887 Robert Giffen wrote:

> ... the working-classes of the United Kingdom have enjoyed a great improvement in wages in the last fifty years, an improvement roughly estimated at 50 to 100 per cent; there has been a ... fall in the prices of the principal articles of general consumption, ... the condition of the masses has in fact improved vastly, as is shown by the diminished rate of mortality, the increased consumption per head of tea, sugar, and the like articles ...
>
> The conclusion ... is, that what has happened to the working-classes ... is a revolution ..., having substituted for millions of people, ... who were constantly on the brink of starvation, and who suffered untold privations, new millions of artisans and fairly well-paid labourers.

In the second half of the nineteenth century there were a number of discoveries which affected the nation's health: Lister, Pasteur (Picture 8) and other scientists discovered the causes of and remedies for some diseases. Doctors were better trained after the setting up of the British Medical Association and nurses and midwives were better qualified as a result of the work of Florence Nightingale. New and better equipment helped most of them in their work.

The National Health Service
Nineteenth-century governments had been concerned with the environment in which people lived. They had passed laws which led to the beginning of slum clearance, council house building; by 1900 every town had a Medical Officer of Health, a proper system of refuse collection and main drainage, an organised water supply. Thousands of people still lived in slums (Picture 7). Indeed, even in 1970, many thousands still do – it is not possible quickly to clear away the results of a century of unregulated building. But a start had been made

9 Peabody buildings, Westminster, 1869

on setting aside part of the increased national income to provide better living conditions; towns became more pleasant places in which to live and work.

The Liberal Government (1906–14) took a major step forward when it decided that another duty of a government was to provide money and services for people in need, e.g. for old people (Chapter 7, Picture 8), and for some unemployed people (Chapter 2, Picture 7). They also passed the first National Insurance Act which dealt with the setting up of a Health Service. Every manual worker earning less than £160 per year had to pay 4d per week into a National Insurance Fund out of which the government would pay doctors to look after him when sick as well as paying him 10/– per week when he was off work owing to sickness (Picture 6). This service did nothing for the worker's wife and family, nor did it do anything for his own dental or optical treatment. It said nothing about paying hospital fees for the insured man or his family. It was indeed a very limited service. But at least it was a major step forward in that for the very first time the government was going to take some of the nation's income (in taxes and employers' contributions) and spend that on improving, even if only slightly, the health of some, at least, of the people.

5 The Young Historian

1 Look at Picture 1. Imagine that you are a housebuilder. Explain to someone why you have to charge a rent for the house you build and why you could not build good houses for the working-classes in the middle of the nineteenth century.

2 Look at Pictures 1 and 7. Imagine that you are a low-paid workman. Explain to someone why you cannot afford to pay the rent for a good house.

3 Find out the names of Ministers responsible for slum clearance Acts in 1869 and 1875. Why did these Acts not really help the poor?

4 Look at Picture 1 and Picture 5. Why could the child in the Towers look forward to about twenty years longer life than the child in London?

5 Look at Picture 2. Find out the connection between a poor water supply and the danger of cholera. Who supplies your house with its water supply? Find out from Book 1, Chapter 5, the probable sources of water supply in the 1840s.

6 Look at Picture 7. Many working-class people were living in the suburbs in the 1870s following the development of a good railway system (Chapter 4, Picture 4). Why did the poorer working people not do so?

7 The Doré picture (Picture 7) tries to show how dirty and squalid life was for the poor. Can you suggest why overcrowded houses became dirty?

8 Look at Picture 6. Find out what Lloyd George was promising the people. Find out in particular which members of the family were not going to gain from this Insurance system.

9 Make your own painting of (i) a poor housing area in Victorian England, (ii) a house for a well-to-do family.

6 Government – National and Local

National government 1830

In Book 1, Chapter 6, we saw that the system of elections was very corrupt and that only a small number of people voted for Members of Parliament. We also saw that this system was unpopular – with working-class people who met at Peterloo in 1819, with people who supported movements such as the Cato Street conspiracy and with middle-class people who supported less violent movements for reform.

Reform Acts

In 1832 Parliament passed the first Reform Act which set a national standard qualification for the voters; in borough constituencies every man who paid £10 a year in rates was allowed to vote; in county constituencies freeholders and some leaseholders of property were allowed to vote. The importance of

1 Electioneering at the beginning of the nineteenth century.

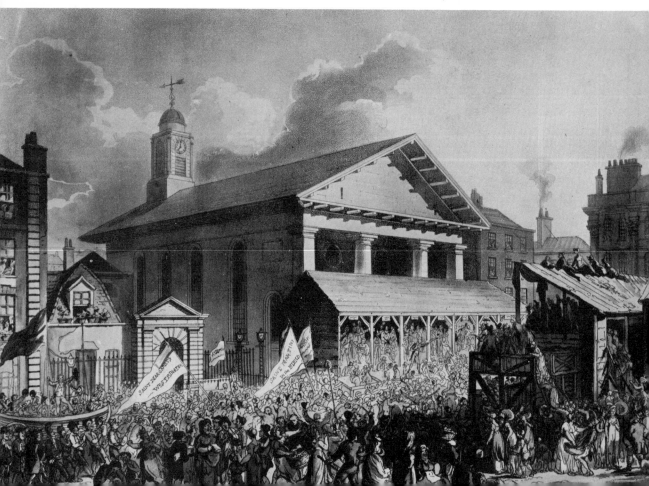

2 A Chartist demonstration on Kennington Common.

this Act was that it admitted thousands of middle-class industrialists and merchants to the vote. By 1840 members of this new class were being elected and Cobden and Bright had a considerable influence on affairs (Chapter 3). By the end of the nineteenth century middle-class MPs had replaced the sons of the aristocracy, particularly in the Liberal Party.

The 1832 Act also began the redistribution of constituencies away from the agricultural South and West towards the industrial Midlands and North. This process continued throughout the nineteenth century. In 1867 all adult male householders in towns were given the vote – and more seats taken from the South and given to the industrial towns. In 1884 agricultural workers were given the vote and a further redistribution of seats took place.

National government's activity

In Book 1, Chapter 6, we saw that government and Parliament had been concerned only with foreign affairs, trade, colonies, and the like. Throughout the period 1830–1914 the scope of government interest widened: at first there were Factory Acts (Chapter 8); then there were the many Health and Housing Acts (Chapter 5); governments passed laws about trade unions (Chapter 8)

3 'A Leap in the Dark', *Punch* cartoon

A LEAP IN THE DARK.

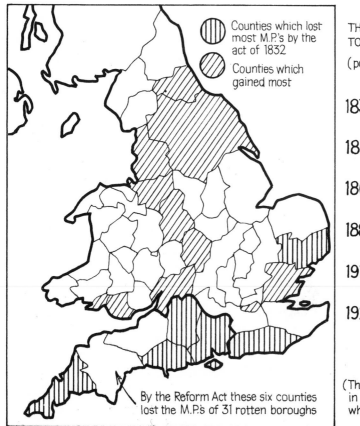

Counties which lost most M.P.'s by the act of 1832

Counties which gained most

By the Reform Act these six counties lost the M.P.'s of 31 rotten boroughs

THE PROPORTION OF VOTERS TO THE TOTAL POPULATION

(population includes children)

1832 Before the Reform Bill

1832 After the Reform Bill

1867 After the Second Reform Act

1884 After the Third Reform Act

1918 After the Representation of the People Act
including votes for women over 30

1928 Votes for all men and women at 21

(The apparent slight decrease in population in 1928 is due to the exclusion of Eire which had its own Parliament after 1922)

4 A map of the constituencies, 1830–1914

and education (Chapter 10). By 1914 the government was beginning to deal with the old, the sick, the unemployed and the young in a small-scale Welfare State.

All this activity meant that taxation had to increase; it also meant that the Civil Service had to grow.

National political parties

The Tory Party was the party of the landed aristocrats and farmers; this is why the Party supported the Corn Laws and why many Tories had followed Disraeli when he quarrelled with Peel (Chapter 3). The middle-class town voters tended to vote for the Whig (later the Liberal) Party which believed in Free Trade. When the working classes were given the vote in 1867 they tended to support the Liberal Party – although it was the Tories who had given them the vote. By the 1880s some working-class voters had begun to realise that neither the Tories nor the Liberals were doing enough to help the lower-paid working classes (Chapter 8). This led some of them to form the Labour Party under the leadership of Keir Hardie. This new Party used its influence on the voters and on Parliament to force the Liberals to pass the laws which started off the modern Welfare State (Chapter 5).

Local government

As we saw in Book 1, Chapter 6, there were 178 boroughs in England and Wales which had their own councils which dealt with such matters as the town market or fair, but had nothing to do with such things as building regulations, street cleansing, etc.

When these things were dealt with it was as a result of a Private Act of Parliament paid for by a few public-spirited people who wanted to improve things in their town. We also saw in Book 1 that there were no councils at all in many parts of England and Wales; industrialists in mining villages and iron towns were their own masters; even the town of Manchester had no council in 1830 despite a population of nearly 200,000.

Reform

In 1835 the government passed the Municipal Corporations Act which abolished all the old councils, fixed a national standard for voting – every ratepayer was allowed to vote in local elections – and divided every Chartered Borough into wards with three councillors for each ward. The Act also made it possible for non-Chartered Boroughs (such as Manchester) to apply to Parliament for a Charter which would allow the new towns to have an elected council; Manchester got its Charter in 1838.

But no one thought that it was the job of even these reformed councils to look after living conditions in the towns. When the problem of Poor Law was dealt with in 1834 the government ordered the election in each town of a Board of

49

5 Election issues, 1910. The Liberals had already begun to tax the rich to pay for the beginnings of the Welfare state.

Guardians. In 1848 the Public Health Act ordered the election of a local Board of Health; in 1870 when State Education really started the Education Act ordered the election of a School Board. The Town Council had no control over the Poor Law until 1929; nor over the Health authority or the School Board until 1902. As Dr. Robertson wrote in 1840:

> Until twelve years ago there was no paving and (sewage) Act in the township of Manchester, containing in the year 1831 upwards of 142,000 inhabitants. . . . At the present time the paving of the streets proceeds rapidly in every direction, and great attention is given to the drains. It is gratifying to bear testimony to the zeal of the authorities in carrying on the salutary improvements, especially when it is known that no street can be paved and sewered without the consent of the owners of property. Owing to this cause several important streets remain to this hour disgraceful nuisances. Manchester has no Building Act, and hence, with the exception of certain central streets, over which the Police Act gives the Commissioners power, each proprietor builds as he pleases. New cottages . . . huddled together row behind row, may be seen springing up in many parts. . . . The authorities cannot interfere. A cottage row may be badly drained, the streets may be full of pits, brimful of stagnant water, the receptacle of dead cats and dogs, yet no one may find fault.

However, even in 1835 Town Councils could, if they so wished, take over the work being done by the bodies set up by Private Acts of Parliament dealing with sanitation, water supply and the like. Some councils were very active in

6   Westminster, Millbank Gardens, 1905

7   Tooting Bathing Lake, 1920

8 Manchester town hall opened in 1877

such matters: Manchester Council had got Parliament to pass a law which allowed the Council to own its own gasworks as early as 1840. Other councils, such as the Liverpool Corporation, appointed their own Medical Officers of Health long before Parliament made this compulsory.

By the end of the nineteenth century the work of local councils had grown as Parliament had passed Acts concerning the nation's health, and as councils had become concerned with living conditions in their towns. Some were more active than others and were building council houses for renting to working-class people; others were providing libraries, swimming and boating pools, play-parks, museums. All of them were providing refuse collection and water supplies to make the town a healthier place. Many councils owned their own reservoirs and gasworks; others the town's transport system. They had realised that in a modern society there had to be some social organisation which would prevent the greedy few exploiting the many; they saw the need for some organisation which would provide the non-profit-making amenities which help to make town life a good one. Private enterprise profit-makers built the factories and shops – where money would be made. They did not build libraries, swimming pools, nor lay out public gardens or playing fields. Our local councils have to take part of the nation's income and spend it on such things in order to make life better for us all.

6 The Young Historian

1   Look at the map in Picture 4. Which area of the country had more than its fair share of MPs in 1830. Who do you think approved of this and who were opposed to it?

2   Look at Picture 2. Do you think that all these people were of the same social class? What does it tell you about the support given to the Chartist movement? Can you see the policemen?

3   Find out what six things the Chartists wanted and the dates on which five of the six were granted.

4   Look at Picture 6 and then at Picture 1 in Chapter 5. Write a letter from someone who has just moved into the Millbank houses (Picture 6) to a friend still living in an overcrowded slum.

5   Find out more about the work that Joseph Chamberlain did as Mayor of Birmingham 1873–1876.

6   Look at Picture 5. Why did the Liberals (1906–14) have to increase the amount of tax collected by the government? Who opposed these increases?

7   Look at Picture 8. Find out when your own Town Hall was built, and if it has been enlarged in the last 100 years. Why, do you think, was Manchester's Town Hall larger in 1877 than in 1842? Name the services now provided by your local government which were not provided in 1842.

8   Find out (i) how local government services are paid for, (ii) the name of your own local councillors – there should be three of them.

7 Poverty and Unemployment

Causes and remedies in 1830

In Book 1, Chapter 7, we saw that there were, and are, many reasons why a family might be poor. We saw that the sickness or death of the wage-earner led to a fall in the family income – and so to poverty. We saw that the introduction of new machinery into industry and agriculture (Picture 1) might lead to unemployment and a fall in the family income – and so to poverty. We saw that low wages (Picture 2) meant that working men did not earn enough to provide their families with an adequate amount of food, clothing or shelter.

In 1830 many parishes had their own workhouses to which the poor could go for assistance (Picture 4). In many places the Speenhamland system of Family Income Supplement (Book 1, Chapter 7), had become widely adopted and Justices of the Peace were collecting ever-increasing poor rates to hand on to lowly-paid workers and other poor people.

1   The rich and the poor – 'Capital and Labour' from an early engraving of 1843.

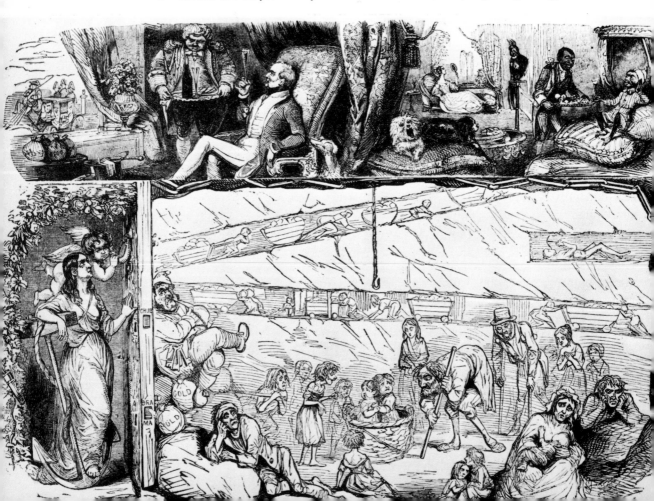

2 Inside a gin palace.

Poor Law Amendment Act, 1834

In 1834 the government was appalled at the continual increase in poor rates –
employers did not raise wage rates, they allowed their lowly-paid workers to
apply to the Justices for assistance. Under the influence of Edwin Chadwick
the government passed a new Poor Law by which every parish was compelled
either to build its own workhouse or to unite with neighbouring parishes to
build a Union workhouse. The Law said that ratepayers were to elect Boards
of Guardians to supervise the running of these workhouses and to administer
the Poor Rate. If sick people applied for Poor Relief the Guardians could give
money or other forms of help to the people involved. But if an able-bodied
person applied for help (because of unemployment or low wages) then the
Guardians were forbidden to give any such assistance; the applicant and his
family had to go into the workhouse where they were separated – men in one
part and women in another, children in a third. Here their living conditions
(food, clothing, shelter) were to be of a poorer quality than that enjoyed by the
lowest-paid worker outside the workhouse. The government feared that if
conditions were made any less harsh the lower-paid workers would all rush into
the workhouse (Picture 4).

This harsh Act was rigorously applied in many places so that children fought

3 Agricultural riots in the 1830s

4 Dinner time at the Parish Workhouse, St. Pancras, 1900

5 Labour yard at Bethnal Green

over scraps of food (Book 1, Chapter 7, Picture 6) and women fought over food intended for the animals on the workhouse farm. In other parts of the country the Act could not be rigorously applied; when 30,000 lace-workers were thrown out of work in Nottingham in 1838 the Board of Guardians could not take them all into the workhouse, and had to give some sort of assistance to the workers in their own homes. Gradually the system was slightly improved. In 1886 the government allowed Guardians to pay unemployed men for doing some sort of work – suggesting stone-breaking or ditch-digging as examples. In 1894 Parliament allowed women and working-class men to stand for election as Guardians. This led to some improvement in conditions in the workhouses – women were allowed underwear, men could have a monthly allowance of tobacco; both men and women were allowed out once a month. But even so conditions in such places were harsh and the poor tried their best to stay away from them, preferring to live in the streets, where they could beg or where they could live on the pennies earned by their children (Picture 7).

Private charity
There were a large number of private attempts to improve life in the nineteenth century; private enterprise tried to provide education for the nation's children (Chapter 10); skilled workers used their high wages to finance their own private schemes for sickness and unemployment benefits (Chapter 8). Private individuals often banded together to force Parliament to do something about a town's insanitary conditions, often at great cost to themselves (Chapter 6, and Book 1, Chapter 6). Similarly with the poor. There are many examples of groups of individuals giving money to try to provide some sort of shelter for the poor (Picture 5), although their efforts were small compared to the size of the problem.

6 Salvation Army shelter in Whitechapel

7 Barefoot matchseller

Societies such as the Quakers and, in particular, the Salvation Army, opened special hostels where the poor could find a cheap meal and bed (Picture 6). However, the Charity Organization Society spoke on behalf of most private charities when it reported:

> It is good for the poor that they should meet all the ORDINARY contingencies of life, relying not upon public or private charity, but upon their own industry and thrift, and upon the powers of self-help. ... The working man does not require to be told that temporary sickness is likely now and then to visit his household; that times of slackness will occasionally come; that if he marries early and has a large family, his resources will be taxed to the uttermost; that if he lives long enough, old age will render him more or less incapable of toil – all these are ordinary contingencies of a labourer's life, and if he is taught that as they arise they will be met by State relief or private charity, he will assuredly make no effort to meet them himself. ... the road to idleness and drunkenness will be made easy to him.

To many Victorians, the causes of poverty lay in the character of the poor and, in particular, in their drinking habits (Picture 2).

Large-scale unemployment
In an agricultural society such as England had been, there was little long-term, large-scale unemployment; a man may have been out of work for a while but he could usually find some employment at harvest time and at other seasons in the year. In the early days of industrialisation many people were put out of work by the new machines; they, too, soon found other work in one of the growing

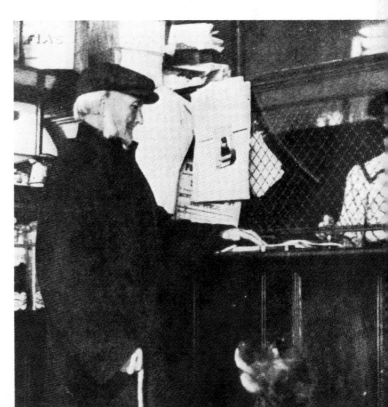

8 One of the first to benefit from the Old Age Pension in London 1909

industries. After 1870, however, as a result of growing foreign competition (Chapter 1, Picture 9), there was the beginning of long-term unemployment in which a man who had lost his job found it very difficult, sometimes impossible, to get another one. This is a problem which we have even in the 1970s; men in Ulster, in parts of Scotland and Wales, have not worked for several years. The problem affects older people rather than the young – who can more easily move from their home town to a developing area. The unemployed (Chapter 2, Picture 7), at first hope, may get violent (Chapter 8, Picture 4), then despair as they join the ranks of the hopeless, and live off the earnings of their children (Picture 7).

Lloyd George and the unemployed

The new Labour Party had twenty-nine MPs in the Parliament of 1906. Their success made Lloyd George and other Liberals realise that something would have to be done about the workers' votes, which might swing to this new Party and so lead to a decline in the Liberal Party. The Liberals, under the influence of the Labour Party, passed the first Old Age Pensions Act (Picture 8) by which old people over seventy were given five shillings a week provided they had no other income. This seems a very small sum to us; it was in fact about one quarter of what unskilled workers earned at the time, and to many old people must have seemed like a gift from heaven. For the unemployed, Lloyd George introduced a National Insurance scheme; men in building, engineering and ship-building industries were forced to pay 2d per week into a National Insurance Fund. They were then entitled to draw seven shillings a week in unemployment benefit if they were out of work. However, after they had drawn this benefit for fifteen weeks in any one year they were then said to have 'run out of entitlement' and so could draw no more and once again they were forced to beg or to apply to the Guardians for help.

This Unemployment Insurance was a very small beginning by the government at providing some sort of help for people who lost their jobs. A rich country could afford to provide this sort of assistance; it could afford to set aside some

9　Queueing outside the pawn shop

part of its income to help the old, the sick and the unemployed. However, in 1911, even the adventurous Lloyd George and the other New Liberals (Chapter 6, Picture 5), did not think that this help should be given to *all* unemployed, or even to *some* of them for very long. They, and most people, were prepared to see the pawnshop continue to be a feature of town life (Picture 9). Here poor families left their few belongings in return for a few shillings needed to pay rent, buy food or coal. Only in post-1945 Britain have pawnshops disappeared as more affluent people have money to buy goods.

Lady Violet Bonham Carter was a child in 1906, when Britain was the richest country in the world. In 1965 she wrote:

> I can remember as a child being haunted by the beggars in the streets, the crossing-sweepers who held out their tattered caps for pennies, the children in rags, fluttering like feathers when the wind blew through them, the down-and-outs sleeping out under the arches or on the benches in the parks with an old newspaper for cover. Those were the days when an agricultural labourer earned and brought up a family on thirteen shillings a week, when a worker in the towns earned eighteen shillings to a pound, to say nothing of the submerged mass of sweated workers down below. . . .

7 The Young Historian

1 Look at Picture 1. What, according to the artist, is the source of the rich man's wealth? Can you find three causes of poverty?

2 Picture 2 shows the interior of one of the many drinking shops in the nineteenth century. Can you say why there were so many of these places? What evidence is there that even young children were used to drinking beer and spirits. When was this made illegal?

3 Look at Picture 3. Find out why the agricultural labourers were rioting in 1830. What name was given at this time to people who smashed up the new industrial machinery? Why did they do this?

4 Look at Pictures 4 and 6. Many of the people in both homes are old. Why do old people have a smaller income than those of middling age? How were these people helped by the Old Age Pensions Act, 1908?

5 Look at Picture 5. Where is Bethnal Green? Find out the main occupation of people in this district in the nineteenth century. Can you suggest why so many of them were unemployed in the 1860s?

6 Look at Picture 7. Why has this child got no shoes? Can you say what effect this would have had on his health?

7 Another job done by boys and girls was that of a crossing sweeper. Read Chapter 16 of *Bleak House* by Charles Dickens, and then either paint or write an account of 'A Day in the Life of the Crossing Sweeper'.

8 Look at Picture 9. Why did many people have to go to the pawnshop each week? Can you say why there are very few such shops now?

8 Trade Unions and Working Conditions

Trade Unions 1830–40

The repeal of the Combination Acts in 1824–25 allowed the formation of trade unions, but forbade them to organise strikes. Until the building of the railway system provided a quick and cheap method of travel, most trade unions were local societies – Sheffield file grinders, Durham miners and Bolton weavers would each form their own union. There were a few national unions (Book 1, Chapter 8, Picture 1), whose existence encouraged Robert Owen, a Lanarkshire factory owner, to try to form a Grand National Consolidated Trade Union which would include all the workmen in all trades throughout the country.

Owen hoped to use the power of this Grand Union to force the government to provide good living conditions and to force employers to provide good working

CAUTION. 9

WHEREAS it has been represented to us from several quarters, that mischievous and designing Persons have been for some time past, endeavouring to induce, and have induced, many Labourers in various Parishes in this County, to attend Meetings, and to enter into Illegal Societies or Unions, to which they bind themselves by unlawful oaths, administered secretly by Persons concealed, who artfully deceive the ignorant and unwary,—WE, the undersigned Justices think it our duty to give this PUBLIC NOTICE and CAUTION, that all Persons may know the danger they incur by entering into such Societies.

ANY PERSON who shall become a Member of such a Society, or take any Oath, or assent to any Test or Declaration not authorized by Law—

Any Person who shall administer, or be present at, or consenting to the administering or taking any Unlawful Oath, or who shall cause such Oath to be administered, although not actually present at the time—

Any Person who shall not reveal or discover any Illegal Oath which may have been administered, or any Illegal Act done or to be done—

Any Person who shall induce, or endeavour to persuade any other Person to become a Member of such Societies,

WILL BECOME

Guilty of Felony,

AND BE LIABLE TO BE

Transported for Seven Years.

ANY PERSON who shall be compelled to take such an Oath, unless he shall declare the same within four days, together with the whole of what he shall know touching the same, will be liable to the same Penalty.

Any Person who shall directly or indirectly maintain correspondence or intercourse with such Society, will be deemed Guilty of an Unlawful Combination and Confederacy, and on Conviction before one Justice, on the Oath of one Witness, be liable to a Penalty of TWENTY POUNDS, or to be committed to the Common Gaol or House of Correction, for THREE CALENDAR MONTHS; or if proceeded against by Indictment, may be CONVICTED OF FELONY, and be TRANSPORTED FOR SEVEN YEARS.

Any Person who shall knowingly permit any Meeting of any such Society to be held in any House, Building, or other Place, shall for the first offence be liable to the Penalty of FIVE POUNDS; and for every other offence committed after Conviction, be deemed Guilty of such Unlawful Combination and Confederacy, and on Conviction before one Justice, on the Oath of one Witness, be liable to a Penalty of TWENTY POUNDS, or to Committment in the Common Gaol or House of Correction, FOR THREE CALENDAR MONTHS; or if proceeded against by Indictment may be

CONVICTED OF FELONY,
And Transported for SEVEN YEARS.

COUNTY OF DORSET,
Dorchester Division

February 22d, 1834.

C. B. WOLLASTON,
JAMES FRAMPTON,
WILLIAM ENGLAND,
THOS. DADE,
JNO. MORTON COLSON.

HENRY FRAMPTON,
RICHD. TUCKER STEWARD,
WILLIAM R. CHURCHILL,
AUGUSTUS FOSTER.

1 Tolpuddle notice

conditions; ultimately he hoped to use his Union to create a sort of Communist state in which there would be no owners of industry at all. These ideas were revolutionary and were opposed by the government and by middle-class people throughout the country. Some employers forced their workpeople to sign 'the document' (Book 1, Chapter 8); others used their influence with magistrates and judges to get them to punish people who endeavoured to start up trade unions (Picture 1). Owen's Union collapsed after the Tolpuddle martyrs were sentenced to exile in Australia and many workers began to support Chartism (Chapter 6, Picture 2) or the Anti-Corn Law League (Chapter 3, Picture 1) as better means of improving their conditions.

Skilled workers' Unions – 1850s

In the late 1840s and 1850s British industry had entered on the second stage of the industrial revolution. The coal, iron, railway engineering and other industries were booming; employers earned huge profits from trade inside the country and from the export trade; they were prepared to pay high wages to skilled workmen who made the iron, dug the coal, built and maintained the machines. By this time also, a generation of workmen were growing up who had never known life in the village (Book 1, Chapter 1, Pictures 1, 2, 3 and 4). They were the first generation of men born and bred in town life. They knew no other and wanted to improve this life.

These skilled, highly-paid workmen united in trade unions which grew into national societies as various local groups amalgamated. The best known

2   Tea time in a skilled worker's home, 1910

of these Model Unions is the Amalgamated Society of Engineers; its very name suggests a uniting of local societies and also tells us that it was a union of skilled workmen. Other, similar unions were formed for bricklayers, carpenters, weavers and other skilled artisans. Their leaders made their headquarters in London where they met journalists and politicians, and tried to show that trade unionism was not a revolutionary thing as Owen had suggested, but was a private enterprise on the part of the workmen to improve their own life.

Union members paid 1/6d or so each week out of their wages into union funds. Union leaders used these funds to provide their members with weekly payments when sick or out of work; they also provided retirement and widows' pensions. In a word, they provided these skilled workers with their own Welfare State. These workers' high wages allowed them to buy or rent good homes (Picture 2; and Chapter 9, Picture 5) where they and their families lived in comfort. For these men, entitled to vote after 1867 (Chapter 6), the industrial society of nineteenth-century Britain was a prosperous society.

Violence

However, many employers still refused to allow trade unions to start up in their factories and mines. When such efforts were made or when a union organised a strike in support of higher pay, many employers would lock the men out and bring in men (from other districts or from Ireland) to replace the union members. These 'blacklegs' often had to fight their way through union picket lines (Picture 3). Clashes between strikers and the police were common (Picture 4) and in 1865–66 a series of clashes in Sheffield led to several deaths, and a government Commission to inquire into the whole question of trade unionism.

At the same time the trade unions had asked for a Commission to examine the legal position of trade unions after a judge had decided that a trade union could not prosecute a dishonest official who had run away with union funds. The unions wanted a change in the law which would allow them to own property and to take court action if they wanted to. In 1868 the leaders of trade unions

4 Railway strikers at Motherwell, Scotland, clashing with police

[1] *Beehive*, June 13, 1868.

PROPOSED CONGRESS OF TRADES COUNCILS

AND OTHER

Federations of Trades Societies.

MANCHESTER, FEBRUARY 21st, 1868.

FELLOW-UNIONISTS,

The Manchester and Salford Trades Council having recently taken into their serious consideration the present aspect of Trades Unions, and the profound ignorance which prevails in the public mind with reference to their operations and principles, together with the probability of an attempt being made by the Legislature, during the present session of Parliament, to introduce a measure detrimental to the interests of such Societies, beg most respectfully to suggest the propriety of holding in Manchester, as the main centre of industry in the provinces, a Congress of the Representatives of Trades Councils and other similar Federations of Trades Societies. By confining the Congress to such bodies it is conceived that a deal of expense will be saved, as Trades will thus be represented collectively; whilst there will be a better opportunity afforded of selecting the most intelligent and efficient exponents of our principles.

It is proposed that the Congress shall assume the character of the annual meetings of the British Association for the Advancement of Science and the Social Science Association, in the transactions of which Societies the artizan class are almost entirely excluded; and that papers, previously carefully prepared, shall be laid before the Congress on the various subjects which at the present time affect Trades Societies, each paper to be followed by discussion upon the points advanced, with a view of the merits and demerits of each question being thoroughly ventilated through the medium of the public press. It is further suggested that the subjects treated upon shall include the following :—

    1.—Trades Unions an absolute necessity.
    2.—Trades Unions and Political Economy.
    3.—The Effect of Trades Unions on Foreign Competition.
    4.—Regulation of the Hours of Labour.
    5.—Limitation of Apprentices.
    6.—Technical Education.
    7.—Arbitration and Courts of Conciliation.
    8.—Co-operation.
    9.—The present Inequality of the Law in regard to Conspiracy, Intimidation, Picketing, Coercion, &c.
   10.—Factory Acts Extension Bill, 1867: the necessity of Compulsory Inspection, and its application
        to all places where Women and Children are employed.
   11.—The present Royal Commission on Trades Unions: how far worthy of the confidence of the
        Trades Union interest.
   12.—The necessity of an Annual Congress of Trade Representatives from the various centres of
        industry.

All Trades Councils and other Federations of Trades are respectfully solicited to intimate their adhesion to this project on or before the 6th of April next, together with a notification of the subject of the paper that each body will undertake to prepare; after which date all information as to place of meeting, &c., will be supplied.

It is also proposed that the Congress be held on the 4th of May next, and that all liabilities in connection therewith shall not extend beyond its sittings.

Communications to be addressed to MR. W. H. WOOD, Typographical Institute, 29, Water Street, Manchester.

By order of the Manchester and Salford Trades Council,

                          S. C. NICHOLSON, PRESIDENT.
                          W. H. WOOD, SECRETARY.

5 First TUC congress

in Salford called a national conference of representatives of all trade unions (Picture 5) and although the representatives of the older, skilled unions did not attend, this is regarded as the first meeting of the Trades Union Congress.

New Unions

No one at the Congress and no leader of a skilled union thought that it was any part of his job to form unions for the unskilled workers. The skilled workers accepted the employers' ideas about society – that everyone should look after himself and that no one had any responsibility for people less well off than himself. The skilled workers were grateful to the Liberal and Tory Parties which, between 1868 and 1875, passed laws which safeguarded their funds, allowed them to strike, and to picket while on strike. Meanwhile, the unskilled workers were ignored. London Dock workers queued up at the dock gates waiting for work (Picture 6) for which they got 4d an hour; gasworkers shovelled coal and coke in the country's gasworks for twelve hours a day and earned about £1 a week; workers in match and candle factories earned 2d an hour. While the skilled worker, with his £2–£3 a week, could have a high standard of living, the unskilled, lowly-paid worker could afford only poor, inadequate housing (Picture 7); his children had to work (Chapter 7, Picture 7, and Picture 10 here); his wife and children had poor quality clothing, often picked up out of dustbins (Chapter 9, Picture 8).

In the late 1880s Annie Besant organised a union for the girls in Bryant and May's match factory. Will Thorne organised the London gasworkers and, most important of all, Ben Tillet and Tom Mann organised the unskilled London dockers into a Dockers' Union. All these unskilled unions succeeded by strikes in forcing the employers either to shorten the working day or to increase wages, or both. London Dockers were paid 6d an hour after their strike.

But even so their members could not afford the high subscriptions of the skilled unions; these unions could not build up the funds required to provide a welfare service for their members. Nor did these members' increased wages allow them to buy or rent decent housing. It was these unskilled workers who first realised that if their living conditions were to improve and if they were to have sickness and unemployment payments then Parliament would have to pass a series of laws. Since neither the Liberal nor the Tory Party showed any inclination to do so, these workers helped to form the Labour Party. The skilled workers joined this Party only when the Taff Vale case put their large funds in danger.

These new unions for unskilled workers were much larger than the national unions of skilled workers – since there were more unskilled than skilled. They were also more militant – since they had to try to force employers to give them better conditions while the skilled men could afford to negotiate with employers. Many of the leaders of these new unions had been affected by the writings of Karl Marx and other socialists who advocated state control of industry; some of them had become 'syndicalists' who believed that the workers in an industry should own and run it. These ideas developed in the period 1910–14, leading to huge strikes (Picture 8) and to the formation of the Triple Alliance 1914, which was to lead to the General Strike in 1926.

Working conditions

The first effective Factory Act was passed in 1833 when the government appointed four Factory Inspectors to see that the terms of the Act were obeyed by employers. In the 1830s and 1840s many attempts were made to get children out of textile mills (Book 1, Chapter 1, Picture 6; and Book 1, Chapters 2 and 8). By 1850 the government had fixed the working day in textile mills as 10 hours for men

7 Poor East End kitchen, 1912

8 Transport strike of 1916—Ben Tillett addressing a crowd

9 A tailor's sweat shop in the East End, 1904

10 Children at work (a) in the brick fields: (b) underground in a coal mine

and women. In other industries the workers had to wait until 1875 when Disraeli's government extended the laws from the textile mills to all industries. However, right throughout this period until 1914, children worked – if not in the mines, then in brickyards or on the streets (Chapter 7, Picture 7). Many thousands of workers did not work in factories but in their own homes or in attics provided by employers. These 'sweated' workers (Picture 9, and Chapter 7) had to wait until 1908 before the government passed a Trades Boards Act which tried to regulate conditions in such industries.

In a richer country a greater number of people were beginning to share in the good things of life. However, in 1914 over one-third of the population were still very poor, with insufficient income to buy food, clothing and shelter. The national income was still not being shared out very equally.

8 The Young Historian

1   When did the Government make it illegal for children to work underground. Write a letter giving an account of your day's work as a child worker in the mine. (See also Chapter 7.)

2   Look at Picture 10(a). Why did parents allow their children to do such work? Find out from Chapter 7 two other occupations in which young children worked towards the end of the nineteenth century.

3   Look at Picture 3. Why were the strikers trying to stop the blackleg labour going to work? With which group did the police side? Why did this often lead to bloodshed?

4   Look at Pictures 2 and 7. Which was the home of (i) the skilled worker, and (ii) the unskilled worker? Write a letter from the poorer child telling of his visit to the home of the better-off child.

5   Look at Picture 6. Why were many of the dockers not going to get work on the day this was taken? Find out something about the work of Ben Tillet and Tom Mann, and the present name of the union they started in 1889.

6   Paint or draw one of the Pictures 4, 6 or 10, as part of your frieze on life in an industrial town.

7   Look at Picture 9. Why did Factory Inspectors not visit homes such as these? What evidence is there that this family was getting only a low income? What effect did such work have on the health of the family?

8   Find out (i) when the law forbade children under 14 to go to work and forced them to stay at school, (ii) when the Trades Boards Act was passed concerning the 'sweated' industries.

9 Women and the Family

Upper-class families

During this period (1830–1914) Britain became the richest country in the world and the nation's income grew every year. Among those who gained most from this continual expansion were the ever-increasing numbers of rich families – industrialists who owned factories and mines (Chapter 7, Picture 1); shareholders in railway and other companies (Chapter 2, Pictures 4 and 5); merchants and shopkeepers (Chapter 1, Picture 7), as well as government officials and professionally qualified men (Chapter 2, Picture 6). An ever-increasing number were able to buy large houses (Chapter 5, Picture 5) where they brought up large families with the aid of an army of servants (Pictures 3 and 4).

In these families the mother was often little more than a 'beautiful bird in a gilded cage'; she ordered the servants, she drove out in a carriage, she dressed in

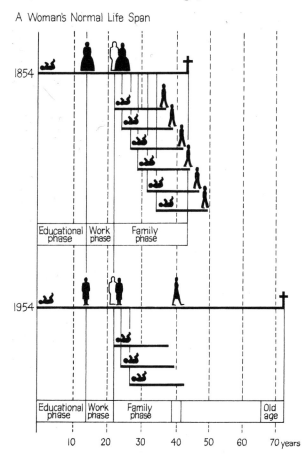

1 Graph showing family sizes

2 Dining at home

3 Lady showing a guest the servant's quarters

4 Men servants in the early 1900s

expensive clothes bought in one of the new large shops (Chapter 1, Picture 7). But she had little, if any, freedom; she was subordinate to her husband (Picture 2). Until 1882 she was not even allowed to own property – even if it were left to her in a parent's will, her 'property' became that of her husband. For her sons, life was better; they went away to one of the public schools (Book 1, Chapter 10, Picture 1) and later started off on a career of their own. For her daughters, life was bleak; they were usually educated at home (Book 1, Chapter 10, Picture 2). Most girls knew that marriage was to be their career and both they and their parents spent their time and effort at husband-catching (Picture 10).

However, not every girl managed to catch a husband; many men emigrated (Picture 7) to the colonies; many men were killed in the wars fought in Asia and Africa as the Empire was won; some women, indeed, did not wish to marry. What was to happen to the girls who couldn't or wouldn't marry? Until the 1850s or so, such girls had been expected either to become 'companions' to older, rich women or to become 'aunts' to the families of their married sisters. Some had become governesses (Book 1, Chapter 10, Picture 2). Then in the middle of the nineteenth century a small number of middle-class women decided that they were going to break out of the traditional way of life and obtain jobs, become properly qualified and live a life of their own. One famous woman who did this was Florence Nightingale; you can read Cecil Woodham Smith's *Lady with the Lamp* and see the difficulty she had in persuading her parents to let her become a nurse. Other women started schools for middle-class girls so that they could become qualified; Miss Emily Davies started the first women's College (Girton) at Cambridge in 1869. Elizabeth Garrett Anderson fought against male prejudice to become the first British woman doctor.

The attempts to become 'emancipated' or free to do what they wanted were helped by the development of new industries (Chapter 2, Picture 6) in which there was work for qualified women workers. Other women found work in offices (Chapter 2, Picture 8) and in the Civil Service (Chapter 7). The development of new technologies and inventions, such as typewriter and telephone, helped to provide work suitable for educated women. However, it was still true

73

5 Skilled workers' wives on an outing 1912

in 1914 that most men and women thought that 'a woman's place is in the home' and those women who went to work were considered bold.

Working-class families

No one thought it bold of a working-class girl to go to work; they had always worked, although Factory and Mines Acts forbade them certain types of work (Chapter 8, Picture 9). For working-class women, emancipation meant the freedom not to go to work – which they achieved when their skilled husbands won sufficient wages to allow the family to live well without depending on the mother's wages (Chapter 8, Picture 2; and Picture 5 here). However, the number of skilled workers was small even in 1914. Few men earned the £2–£3 a week of skilled workers. Most had only £1 or 30/– a week. Their wives' work was essential if they were to stay out of the pawnshop (Chapter 7, Picture 9). The poor (Picture 8) needed the mother's wages as unemployment (Chapter 2, Picture 7) became more common; even so, their living conditions were often very poor (Chapter 5, Picture 7) and their children were compelled to work (Chapter 7, Picture 7; and Chapter 8, Picture 10). Even so their homes, furniture and food were of a much lower standard than those of the skilled workers' families (Chapter 8, Picture 7). Wal Hannington recalls in *Never on our Knees*:

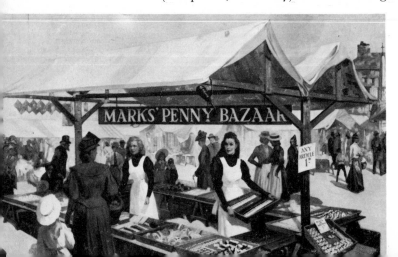

6 Marks and Spencer's first stall, the 'Penny Bazaar' in Leeds market in 1884

When I left school in 1910 at the age of fourteen I was no stranger to hard work. Since the age of ten I had worked part-time in the evenings after school and all day on Saturdays. Shops were open until 10 pm during the week and midnight on Saturdays. I had one job at a local grocer's where I worked for four hours on two or three evenings in the week and was paid 4d per evening. On Saturdays I worked all day at the shop from 9 in the morning until 10 at night, and was paid 1/– for that day's work.

Many girls from the working-classes found work as servants (Picture 3). By 1851 there were already 1½ million domestic servants in Britain. Towards the end of the century there were increasing opportunities for such girls to find work in the growing number of shops (Picture 6) particularly when large shops were opened in town and city centres (Chapter 1, Picture 7).

Large families

In the middle of the Victorian period it was common for women to have six, eight, or more children. In 1870 the average number of children per family was 5·8. Since the expectation of life was only about forty-two years in 1870, there was little point in spending much time or money on the education of girls. By the time the youngest child was off their hands they would be too old or too tired to take up a career or would be near to death.

Towards the end of the nineteenth century some middle-class families began to have smaller numbers of children. The young parents had been brought up in great comfort (Chapter 1, Picture 4; Chapter 11, Picture 2) and they wanted to have such comforts – and more – for themselves. They wanted to spend more on the education of their sons; they wanted to enjoy holidays and entertainment. At the same time their incomes were not rising as rapidly as incomes had risen earlier in the century. They were the victims of the fall in profits that came with

7 Emigration from England to Canada, 1870

8   Barefoot children in London

the great depression (Chapter 1, Picture 9). They were also forced to pay higher wages for their servants – who could get other jobs in shops or offices. This move towards the smaller family did not affect the size of working-class families until the 1920s and 1930s. In this, as in most other things, the habits of the upper classes were adopted at a later date by the lower classes.

Votes for women
In 1913, A. G. Gardiner noted:

> The demand of the women for the vote is fundamentally different from the demand of the man for the extension of the franchise to himself. His protest is against a discrimination between those who own much and those who own little. His manhood is not insulted by the discrimination; he is only injured as an individual or as a member of a class. But the woman's claim springs from deeper sources. It is not political, but elemental. She claims the vote, not as an instrument merely, though it is that too, but as a flag – the flag of her freedom from the sex-subjection of the past. The vote to her is what the removal of the bandages from the feet is to the Chinese woman. It is not only a release from physical or political restraint; it is a symbol of spiritual emancipation.

Many women believed in 'emancipation' – they believed that women should be as free as men. However, they were not free to become lawyers (until 1919); they were not allowed to vote (until 1918). Few parents believed that they

9   Mrs Pankhurst being arrested outside Buckingham Palace in May 1914

10   The drawing class—From *Punch*, 1885

should spend as much on the education of girls as on that of boys – indeed some parents still believe this today. Mrs Pankhurst (Picture 9) and her supporters chained themselves to railings, broke windows, interrupted political meetings, threw leaflets down on to Members of the House of Commons – all to draw attention to their demand that women should be allowed to vote. They were opposed by most men and by many women. Mrs Fawcett, another emancipationist, believed that women should be treated as equals with and by men. She noted that women would get the vote when they had already got their economic freedom and economic equality with men. She and her supporters were in a sense more important than Mrs Pankhurst who wanted women to have the vote; they wanted women to have equality in every field of life.

9 The Young Historian

1 Look at the graphs in Picture 1. How many children did 611 women have if they married between 1870 and 1879? What was the number of children born to 612 women married between 1900 and 1909? What does this tell you about the size of families at the beginning of the twentieth century?

2 How many children are in the dining room in Picture 2? Can you say who might be looking after the younger children? Where might the children of school age be?

3 How many servants are in Picture 4? Each of these cost their employer about £50 a year in wages and keep. Can you say why there are fewer servants today than there were in 1900?

4 Find out when the telephone was invented. How did this affect the chances of a girl finding a job? Can you name other inventions that have helped women to find work?

5 Look at Picture 5 and then at Picture 9 in Chapter 8. Can you say why the women in the last picture didn't go on outings such as this (Picture 5)? Write a letter that might have been written by one of the poorer women (Chapter 8, Picture 9) who had been taken on an outing.

6 Look at Picture 6. Find out when Marks opened his first stall. Why did he sell everything for 1d? Look at Chapter 1, Picture 7. What sort of people used Marks' stall, and what sort of people went to the new shops?

7 Look at Picture 7. Many people emigrated to Australia, America, Canada and New Zealand. Few, if any, went to Nigeria or Ghana. Why? Write a letter from an emigrant to Canada to a friend still living in London or Birmingham.

8 Look at Picture 9. Find out the names of two different groups which campaigned for votes for women. Write your account of the arrest of Mrs Pankhurst.

10 Education

Schools in 1830

In Book 1, Chapter 10, we saw that there was a great variety of schools; for the very rich there were the boarding schools such as Eton and Rugby; for the middle classes there were the old grammar schools or the dame schools; for the poor there were charity schools and the new monitorial schools run by the Anglican National Society or by the Non-Conformist Bible and Foreign Society. We also saw that in spite of numerous debates in Parliament the Government played no part in educating any of the nation's children.

1830–1870

During this period Britain became the workshop of the world, and her national income grew each year. Some of this money was taken by the ever-increasing numbers of middle-class people (Chapter 1, Picture 4; Chapter 2, Picture 6; Chapter 7, Picture 1, and Chapter 9, Picture 2) to pay for the education of their sons – and later, of their daughters. These new middle-class people wanted to imitate the lives of the old aristocracy and so they sent their sons to boarding schools. Since the old schools could not take all the applicants from the new middle class, many new schools had to be opened and the children travelled by the new railway system from their homes in industrial areas to schools in the rural South and West.

These parents paid high fees for the education of their children. Other middle-class parents could not afford such fees. They did, however, have enough money to pay for the building of new grammar schools (Picture 6) and for the opening of many smaller private schools to which their children went as day pupils. The richer children usually went on to university after the age of eighteen; the grammar school children usually left school at sixteen to take up a career in one of the professions or in business.

Many of the skilled working classes (Chapter 1, Picture 5; Chapter 8, Picture 2; and Chapter 9, Picture 5), were able to afford the 2d or 4d to send their children to the less expensive private or dame schools which opened in the industrial towns. They and other people thought that the monitorial schools were for the 'poor' only. In 1833 the government at last began to play a part in the education of these poorer children. They set aside £20,000 a year for the two Societies to help them build more schools – although most of the money required still had to come from voluntary subscriptions and children's fees (Book 1, Chapter 10). By 1860 the government was giving over £2 million per year to the societies and hundreds of Church schools had been opened. Inside, most of these schools

consisted of a schoolroom (Picture 1) where sometimes a master was helped by monitors; sometimes two or more masters taught side by side.

There was no fixed starting age for schoolchildren, nor was there any compulsion on them to attend once they had begun school. Some children started when they were seven; some when eleven – depending upon their parents' ability to do without the wages the children might have earned (Chapter 7, Picture 7; and Chapter 8, Picture 10).

Even when they had started, schoolchildren took time off to help with the harvest (Chapter 3, Picture 5) and absence was common whenever the weather was bad or when an area was attacked by disease (Chapter 5, Picture 2).

State elementary education, 1870–1902

In 1870 the Franco-Prussian war was fought in Europe; Prussia's success led to the formation of a united Germany. One of the main reasons for the success of the smaller Prussia in this war was that she had a compulsory system of education for all children. Some people began to realise that if Britain wanted to remain a leading power she would have to do something similar.

At the same time, industry was beginning to get more complicated and there was a need for more highly-qualified workpeople (Chapter 2, Pictures 4, 5 and

2   A Board school in Leicester

Department	Average attendance	For payment after deduction under Art 4	Presented for examination	Passes on Examination				For payment after deduction under Art 4	Infants under 6	For payment after deduction under Art 4	Half Time Art. 47(b)
				R.	W.	A.	Total passes				
Boys or mixed under Master	43	43	36	34	30	34	98	98	7	7	—
Girls or mixed under Mistress	35	35	27	22	26	25	73	73	6	6	—
Infants											
Total Day School	78	78	63	56	56	59	171	171	13	13	—

Department	On average attendance	On examination	On attendance only		Total £ s. d.
			Infants under 6	Half time Scholars under Art 47(b)	
Boys or mixed	8 12 -	13 14	2 5 6	—	23 18 10
Girls or mixed	7 -	9 14 8	1 19 -		18 13 8
Infants					
Total Day School	15 12 -	22 16 -	4 4 6	—	42 12 6
Evening					

3 Payments by results

8). Some of these would come from the boarding and grammar schools and would be the professional leaders of industry (Chapter 2, Picture 6). But their work would be useless without more qualified men at the machines and on the factory floor. So some people began to realise that if Britain wanted to continue to be a leading industrial power we would have to spend more on education.

W. E. Forster was responsible for the 1870 Education Act which split the country into thousands of School Districts. In each district there was to be an elected School Board which could collect a School Rate, build Board Schools (Picture 2) side by side with the older Society schools. At first the Board School children had to pay small fees and the government did not make attendance compulsory. Gradually, over the next twenty years, fees were abolished, while attendance was made compulsory – at least until the age of twelve – although some children were allowed to leave school for part of the day. These half-

4 A factory inspector visiting half-timers, 1881

5 Drill classes in school playground in 1906

timers worked either in the morning or in the afternoon, and went to school for the other half of the day (Picture 4).

In these schools the lessons were often boring (Picture 7) and the main job of teachers was to show children how to behave properly. Many of them had no idea how to behave. Teachers had to be very strict (Picture 5) and could not allow the freedom of movement and expression which are enjoyed in schools today. Many of the children had had to fight their way to survival in the streets (Chapter 9, Picture 8; and Chapter 7, Picture 7). One Inspector's report quoted by Mary Sturt in *The Education of the People*, said:

> In many instances a large proportion of the scholars are of the 'street Arab' class, who are now for the first time brought under the influence of discipline and good example. Some were hardy enough, some were very intelligent in appearance, some were cowed and sly but vicious, and some were dulled into semi-imbecility by hunger, disease and ill-usage. Almost all, when spoken to, winced in expectation of a blow. Not one knew the alphabet or had any idea of order and discipline or of obeying orders, and none could attend for more than five minutes.

If you compare the first elementary schoolchildren with children in the same school at later dates you will appreciate some of the problems of the teachers (Picture 8).

82

Higher Education

These Board schools were supposed only to provide elementary education. The Government set up a separate system of technical schools to which fee-paying children could go after the age of eleven; some of the Board schools persuaded children to stay on until they were thirteen and fourteen, and teachers helped these children to pass examinations in technical drawing and other subjects so that they too could get better jobs. Meanwhile, the grammar schools continued as private, fee-paying schools.

In 1902 the Government decided to tidy up this administrative muddle. They abolished the old School Boards and made County Schools responsible for all forms of education of children after the age of eleven. Borough Councils were responsible for elementary education; Counties could build their own grammar and technical schools and could charge fees to pupils. They could also take over any of the old grammar schools which wanted to get State money. In 1907 the Government passed a law which provided that any school getting State money would have to keep one-quarter of its places for children from the elementary schools – and so the eleven-plus was invented to pick out the elementary school-children who would join the fee-paying middle-class children in the grammar school.

If you read the opening chapters of the autobiographies of Charles Chaplin or Herbert Morrison (later Labour Home Secretary), you will see how difficult life was for children at the beginning of this century. Herbert Morrison's father was a London policeman, and not one of the poorer paid or unemployed. Even so, Morrison recalls: '(In 1901) the time was coming when my education was to be regarded as completed. Secondary education was hardly thought of by parents of my class and time.'

6 The new Grammar School at Reading, 1871

7 Elementary school classroom in the early 1900s

8 Three pictures showing children from the same school in 1894, 1924 and 1952

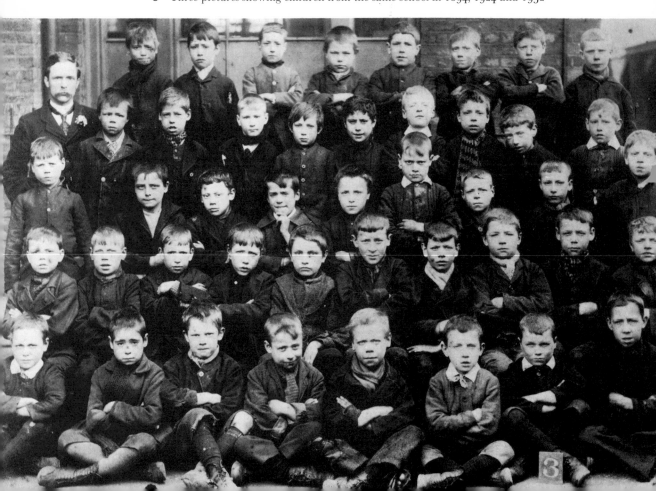

The nation's income and education

If the nation's income was to continue to grow then the country would have to have more and more qualified workpeople to run the new industries (Chapter 2, Pictures 4 and 5). This would mean increased spending by Government on universities, technical colleges, grammar schools and elementary schools. On the other hand, as the country grew richer so it could afford to set aside some of the increased income to pay for such education. One of Britain's failures at the end of the nineteenth century was that we did not spend as much money on State education as did the Americans or Germans. This is one reason for their greater success in the modern industrial world.

10 The Young Historian

1 Picture 2 is typical of the many Board Schools built after 1870. What other building does this remind you of? Find out who ran most of the elementary schools before 1870.

2 Look at the extract in Picture 3. Find out when such a system of paying teachers was stopped.

3 Look at Picture 4. Why is the Inspector visiting these children? When was the school leaving age fixed at (i) ten, (ii) eleven, (iii) twelve?

4 Look at Picture 5. How does it differ from the PE lesson that you have today? Which would you prefer?

5 Look at Picture 6. What sort of children went to schools such as this?

6 Look at Picture 7. Where is the teacher's desk. Why should discipline have to be very strict in this school?

7 Look at Picture 8. Which group of children look the healthiest? Can you suggest three reasons for this improvement? Imagine a conversation between a child from the first and third group. What would they have to say about (i) school meals, (ii) secondary schools, (iii) medical inspection?

8 Look at Picture 7. How do arrangements in this school differ from those in the monitorial school (Book 1, Chapter 10, Picture 5) and from those in nineteenth-century Board Schools (Picture 2).

11 Leisure and Entertainment

Club life

The aristocracy had always had their gambling and drinking clubs, and the rich middle-class (Picture 1) .formed their own, where they met, ate, drank and gambled. Other clubs were formed for more serious matters – for debating, for amateur scientists, for camera enthusiasts, etc. The working-class also started working men's clubs where they could get books, newspapers, hear lectures, as well as play a variety of indoor games. Some of these clubs developed into education institutes, one becoming Birkbeck College at London University.

Sport

The rich middle-class enjoyed an increasing amount of leisure time: they also had large houses with large gardens. Here they were able to entertain each other at tennis parties (Picture 2) or they met to go to the cycling club, cricket game or the amateur football match. The skilled working-classes again imitated their social superiors by starting off their own football teams – sometimes centred on a works (as was Arsenal); sometimes on a Church, as was Everton. As the

1   Young swells

2 A tennis party—drawn by Gerald du Maurier

railways developed so games between distant clubs became possible; crowds could be brought to watch these games – either by train or by the new electric trams.

Theatres
Most cities and towns had at least one theatre to which the companies could travel by the railway. Here the middle- and working-classes could enjoy watching great actors such as Irving or Ellen Terry and their imitators performing in

3 Derby Day, 1871

4   Pierrots at Scarborough in August, 1907

5   Football match, 1891

6 Inside a Victorian public house

7 Astley's Amphitheatre in 1843

plays by Shakespeare, or in bloodthirsty or romantic melodramas. Larger towns had a music hall (Picture 7) where singers, conjurers, trapeze artists and other performers appeared. In some of these halls the management provided meals as well as entertainment. By the end of the century the music-hall artists such as Marie Lloyd or Dan Leno were as famous as today's 'pop' stars, and their songs were sung or the tunes whistled, by thousands of their fans. By the end of the period the cinema was presenting moving pictures – though without any sound. Technology was helping to provide a new form of entertainment.

Travel

During this period there was a steady growth in the number of newly-rich industrialists and shopkeepers. These people imitated the way of life of the older landed aristocracy – they bought houses in the countryside, they entertained lavishly in their homes, they employed servants and sent their sons to boarding schools. Similarly, they began to travel abroad – as the aristocracy had always done. To help them to do so Thomas Cook organised his travel agency and, using the railways and steamships, enabled the new middle-classes to explore the cities of Europe as well as the remains of old civilisations in Europe and Africa.

The skilled working-class enjoyed a high standard of living and one of their pleasures was to take a trip to the seaside (Chapter 4, Picture 8) or to the country-side (Chapter 9, Picture 5). For the unskilled working-class there was no such pleasure. They were too poor to buy sufficient food (Chapter 1, Picture 6) or clothing (Chapter 9, Picture 8), let alone spend money on theatre or railway tickets. For them there were the brutal, but cheap forms of public entertainment (Book 1, Chapter 11) and the pub (Picture 6). Here for a penny (they were promised) they could get drunk and forget the miserable conditions in which they lived. In *London Labour and London Poor*, Henry Mayhew described the 'Amusements of Costermongers':

> Their leisure is devoted to the beer-house; the dancing room and the theatre. Home has few attractions. Skittles is a favourite amusement; the game is always for beer, but betting goes on. A fondness for sparring and boxing lingers among the rough members of some classes. 'Twopenny hops' are much resorted to by the costermongers, men and women, boys and girls. The numbers present at these 'hops' vary from thirty to one hundred of both sexes, their ages being from fourteen to forty-five. There is nothing of the leisurely style of dancing – half a glide and half a skip – but vigorous and laborious capering. The hours are from half-past eight to twelve, sometimes to one or two in the morning, and never later than two, as the costermongers are early risers. The other amusements of this class of the community are the theatre and the penny concert, and their visits are almost entirely confined to the galleries of the theatres on the

Surrey-side – the Surrey, the Victoria, the Bower Saloon, and (but less frequently) Astley's. . . . Among the men, rat-killing is a favourite sport. They will enter an old stable, fasten the door, and then turn out the rats. Or they will find out some unfrequented yard, and at night time build up a pit with apple-case boards, and lighting their lamps, enjoy the sport. Nearly every coster is fond of dogs. Some fancy them greatly and are proud of making them fight. Their dog-fights are both cruel and frequent . . .

For those who did not want to spend all their time in a drunken stupor there were the street entertainers. Punch and Judy shows, brass bands as well as barrel organs (Picture 8) travelled the poorer streets, providing some relief for the people from whom the entertainers hoped to pick up a penny.

Racing
The poor and the rich might mingle at the music hall – but each had their separate classes of seating. However, at the races (Picture 3) the aristocrat and the slum dweller might jostle each other as they watched this sport of Kings – a title especially justified when King Edward VII showed a great liking for the sport. Rich and poor alike were shocked when Miss Emily Davison threw herself under the feet of the King's horse at the 1913 Epsom Derby, to draw attention to the demand for 'Votes for Women'.

Leisure and the national income
As a country becomes more industrialised so more people live in towns and cities; they provide ready-made crowds for entertainers – and the technological revolution provides a way of transporting the entertainers and the crowds.

A richer country is also able to afford to spare money to build the theatres and halls, to set aside land for football and tennis, to lay out parks and playing fields. A richer people are able to pay the money to watch entertainers who are not asked to work in agriculture or industry – the productivity of working people is increased so that some can be taken off the production line. Industrial progress is not only the secret of a better standard of home and travel. It is also the key to a better standard of entertainment.

8 A street barrel organ, 1905

11 The Young Historian

1   Look at Picture 1. What social class do these young men belong to? Paint or draw your own idea of the costume that might have been worn by the wives of such men.

2   Look at Picture 2. What social class do these people belong to? Find out when the first public tennis court was opened in your town.

3   Look at Picture 6. Find out when Gladstone's government passed Licensing Laws. What name was given to the Movement which tried to persuade people to drink less?

4   Picture 4 is a picture of Scarborough. How are the people being entertained on the beach? Are there any other forms of entertainment available? Why were places such as Scarborough almost unknown to the working-class?

5   Read the opening chapters of the autobiography of Charlie Chaplin, the famous film star who was born and brought up in London's East End. Why was the barrel organ a popular form of entertainment for poorer people?

6   Picture 5 shows a scene at an early football game. Find out when the Football Association was formed. What was the connection between a half-day's holiday and the growth of professional football?

7   Look at Picture 7. How far does the Music Hall differ from the Theatre (type of entertainment, seating arrangements, etc.)? Find out the names of three male and three female Music Hall stars. Can you suggest why this form of entertainment has died out?

8   Show how the development of the railway affected (i) the growth of professional football, (ii) the appearance of Music Hall stars in different towns in England.

1 Isambard Kingdom Brunel, 1806–1859

2 Sir Edwin Chadwick, 1800–1890

3 William Gladstone, 1809–1898

4 Benjamin Disraeli, Lord Beaconsfield, 1804–1881

5 Florence Nightingale, 1820–1910

6 Thomas Arnold

7 John Bright, 1809–1872

8 Richard Cobden

9 Lord Shaftesbury, 1801–1885

10 David Lloyd George, 1863–1945

11 Sir Robert Peel, 1788–1850

12 Charles Darwin, 1809–1882

Index

Numbers in **bold** type refer to pages on which illustrations appear.